Passionate, credible, inspii  t
and caring.

These chapter titles more 1
Stewart-Rhude. A book of this calibre could only be written by one who
has followed God's call on the rigorous and demanding journey of inner
growth and development, one who has been pushed to the limit in order
to fulfill God's plan and purpose. *The Leadership Edge* is a result of that
journey and comes from Eileen's passion for women today at every level
of leadership. An indispensable book for women who desire to lead at
the edge!

Margaret Gibb
President
Women Alive

It has been my privilege to know Eileen Stewart-Rhude for many
years. We are deeply grateful for her leadership of the WEA Women's
Commission. I am also encouraged that she has taken the time to
record her life-long learnings in this new book. I want to encourage
both women and men to read *The Leadership Edge*. It is filled with
great insights and wisdom from a woman who has faithfully and effectively served Kingdom purposes both in Canada and around the
world.

Dr. Geoff Tunnicliffe
International Director
World Evangelical Alliance

Even though leadership is dangerous, tough and rewarding, little
gets done without it. Eileen Stewart-Rhude in *The Leadership Edge* out-
lines those core issues each of us as leaders need to consider. She breaks
them down into seven dynamics which form the heart and soul of what
it takes to lead. This important book is so helpful, clearly outlined and
instructive on the call to lead. With spark and great content Eileen has

made this delightful book a must-read for anyone interested in this timely subject. Congratulations to Eileen for her outstanding contribution.

Brian C Stiller, DMin
Chancellor
Tyndale University College & Seminary

Practical life lessons from decades of experience and multiple walks of life are contained in this book. Eileen, has her own amazing track record of leading in all types of circumstances, and now she adds extensive interviews from a wide network of Christian leaders she knows to provide an intimate portrait of leadership skills; it's a wonderful "how-to" guide for healing the world.

Lorna Dueck
Executive Producer
Listen Up TV / Columnist

The Leadership Edge

SEVEN KEYS TO DYNAMIC CHRISTIAN LEADERSHIP FOR WOMEN

Eileen Stewart-Rhude

The Leadership Edge: Seven Keys to Dynamic Christian Leadership for Women

Copyright ©2009 Eileen Stewart-Rhude
All rights reserved
Printed in Canada
International Standard Book Number: 978-1-894860-47-5

Published by:
Castle Quay Books
1307 Wharf Street, Pickering, Ontario, L1W 1A5
Tel: (416) 573-3249
E-mail: info@castlequaybooks.com
www.castlequaybooks.com

Copy edited by Marina H. Hofman
Cover design by Essence Graphic Design
Printed at Essence Publishing, Belleville, Ontario

Library and Archives Canada Cataloguing in Publication

Stewart-Rhude, Eileen-
    The leadership edge : seven keys to dynamic Christian
leadership for women / Eileen Stewart-Rhude ; Marina Hofman (editor).
    ISBN 978-1-894860-47-5

    1. Christian leadership. 2. Leadership in women.
I. Hofman, Marina H.   II. Title.
BV652.1.S748 2009   248.8'43   C2009-904747-0

CASTLE QUAY BOOKS

DEDICATION

To my daughters, Mary LuWayne and Marla,
and to my daughters-in-law, Michelle and Beverlie –
each a strong leader in her appointed vocation

And

To my beautiful granddaughters,
Erica, Meredith, Emma, Elanna, and Juliana

My prayer for you, leaders in the making, is that you will strive
to reach The Leadership Edge,
making an impact for the Kingdom of God.

Acknowledgements

So many people come to mind as I begin to write this acknowledgement. First of all, I look back to the seeds that were planted by many Canadian women I taught through the years, as well as young people I influenced and mentored. Often, I was asked, "Will you please write your teachings in a book for us." This is when the dream began. As I travelled, I discovered women all over the world were eager for leadership training. They, too, encouraged me and the seeds were watered.

I am deeply indebted to my daughter, Marla, a published author herself, for her encouragement, professional counsel and hours of editing as the book took shape.

I must express deep gratitude to my 'condo prayer' friends, 12 women who meet weekly and have faithfully prayed for me as I committed myself to the lonely task of writing. Other friends from far and near supported me in the same way. Their notes and calls of encouragement spurred me on.

Women from various age groups, professions, and positions in ministry willingly shared their insights and wisdom with me as the book was in process. I am grateful for their support.

I also express my gratitude to Larry Willard, publisher of Castle Quay Books. It has been a pleasure working with him and his staff.
Finally, I must acknowledge the blessing and guidance of God as each chapter unfolded.

TABLE OF CONTENTS

Introduction

For years, as I have taught leadership for women across Canada and in many nations of the world, I have been asked repeatedly to write a book containing the principles I teach. They are principles from a woman's perspective and address every level of leadership: entry, emerging, developing and advanced. I was sure there must be many leadership books for women on the market, but as I began to investigate, going from one Christian bookstore to another, searching the shelves up and down, there was not one single leadership book written for women. The stores were well stocked with books for Christian men by well-known and popular authors on the subject of effective leadership, both secular and ministry-related, but not one book specifically for women.

To add to my dilemma, while attending a large writers' conference recently, I asked more than a dozen prominent publishers if they had books specifically for women in leadership and written by a woman. They combed through their catalogues and could not find one title. Certainly there is a major gap. They were surprised themselves.

Why is it so important to fill this gap? Women are stepping into leadership at an ever-increasing rate, in church-related ministries, in professions and in the marketplace. They want to lead with excellence and are asking for pertinent leadership training. Working with the Women's Commission of the World Evangelical Alliance, I am also aware of the great need for leadership resources for women at the global level.

Women lead differently from men because of their nature. They are more intuitive, guided and influenced by their feelings. They are nurturers and lead with "influence" power, while men lead with "position" power. Women are collaborative and relational and value the callings and giftedness of others. *The Leadership Edge is* specifically relevant for women.

In writing *The Leadership Edge,* I have drawn on many years of ministry and leadership experience, along with biblical, historical and modern-day examples. These are interwoven throughout the book and set forth both theoretical knowledge and experiential principles.

So, with the request of so many and the urging of my leadership peers and colleagues, I give to you now *The Leadership Edge: Seven Keys to Dynamic Christian Leadership for Women.* These seven keys will open the doors before you to the greatest adventure in leadership you can imagine. In order to reach the leadership edge, you will need the keys of passionate leadership and credible and inspiring leadership. The key of courageous leadership will help you through difficulties along the path to the edge, and the key of nurturing leadership will ensure that there are others travelling with you and following you on your journey. The last two keys, smart leadership and taking care of the leader, offer you great wisdom in practical instruction, preparing you to arrive successfully at the leadership edge.

Part One

PASSIONATE LEADERSHIP

CALLED

Your ears will hear a voice behind you, saying,
"This is the way; walk in it." (Isaiah 30:21)

Passionate leadership is the first key that opens the door to the leadership edge. It begins with the "call of God." Not everyone will hear it in the same manner or at the same age or stage in life, as each call will come uniquely designed for the person receiving it. God will use people or circumstances to confirm the call, whether in the midst of everyday occurrences or through supernatural and dramatic events.

A DIVINE SUMMONS

I remember as if it were yesterday. Sitting in a high school auditorium in a small south-western Ontario town, I listened spellbound to the speaker as he shared his missionary experiences in China. There were about 200 young people at that first Youth for Christ meeting in our area, but it felt like he was speaking directly and personally to me. I hung on his every word, and the more I listened, the faster my heart beat. It was as if I were in China with him, feeling the passion of the millions who were lost without Christ!

At the end of his message, he asked us to bow our heads and invited any who felt God was speaking to them to stand up. By now tears were streaming down my cheeks and I knew God was calling me. I had come to the rally with my sister and her husband, and I wondered what they would think, but I could not stay seated. As I stood to my feet, an indescribable sense of God's presence flooded over me. In the next few moments, in that humble high school auditorium, God and I made a covenant! I was 15 years old, and I have never looked back. God didn't give me a clear map or an outlined plan of my whole life at that time, but I never doubted his call. I was absolutely certain of it.

As a teenager attending missionary services, I loved to sing the hymns of dedication and consecration. Two of my favourites were

I'll go where you want me to go, dear Lord,
O'er mountain, or plain, or sea;
I'll say what you want me to say, dear Lord,
I'll be what you want me to be. (Mary Brown, 1892)

Take my life, and let it be
Consecrated, Lord, to thee. (Frances R. Havergal, 1874)

As I sang these songs and others like them, I sensed the Lord reminding me again of the commitment I made on that special evening in that high school auditorium.

THE CALL CONFIRMED

Many times throughout the following years, my call was confirmed, sometimes through mentors, pastors or friends. They spoke into my life, affirming the call God had placed upon me. Some said they saw special giftings in me that God would use. Trusted friends prayed that I would clearly discern God's unique and specific plan for my life. Over and over again, as I read and studied God's Word and listened to the good preaching of faithful pastors, the Holy Spirit reaffirmed the call I had received as a young teenager. As I write these words now, absolute joy and wonder flood my heart, as they did on that night of God's divine summons.

This is my story. There will never be another exactly like it. Just as each person is unique, so is God's call to each individual.

AN EVER-UNFOLDING AWARENESS OF THE CALL

Sometimes God unfolds his plan for us through circumstances that take place over a period of time, perhaps even years. For some, there is no moment of epiphany or passion but a gradual revelation, an ever-unfolding awareness that God is leading and guiding into his divine purposes. This is how Margaret Jacobs describes God's call for her life.

Margaret, now an ordained minister and member of the International Council of the World Evangelical Alliance (WEA), as well as chair of the WEA Women's Commission, says there was never a time in her life when she was not aware of God's presence. She recalls as a child having a great interest and love for people all over the world. Enthralled by missionary stories, she would pray for the people and places she heard about.

Margaret was thrilled when her parents received a call to the mission field to serve among the Australian Aboriginal people, and this is where she spent her childhood and teenage years. During this time, Margaret had a sense that God was calling her to India, and she faithfully prayed and supported Indian bicycle evangelists. As a young person, she trained as an accountant and took Bible college training by correspondence in order to be prepared for whatever ministry the Lord would open for her.

Margaret recalls, "In these early years of preparation, it was not so much people who spoke into my life, but rather the Holy Spirit, as I prayed and studied the Word of God. In my late teens, I began to search deeply for a closer walk with God, fasting and praying for a revelation from his heart. God gave me a *joy and power* I had never experienced before!" Margaret was surprised to realize that God was not calling her to India but rather to remain and work among the Aboriginal peoples in Australia.

When Margaret was in her early twenties, God used several returned missionaries to mentor and speak powerfully into her life about a Christian worldview. After she served for 20 years in pastoral ministry with her Aboriginal husband, God opened the door for Margaret to minister in many regions of the world, including India and countries in Africa.

"For over 45 years the Lord has been faithfully unfolding his plans and purposes, his calling for my life," she says. Her passionate leadership has given witness to this ever-unfolding call of God.

A CRYSTAL-CLEAR CALLING

It was neither a divine summons from God nor a call that unfolded over time that began the passionate leadership of Lorna Dueck, inspiring her to take amazing risks and believe God for the impossible. It was the voice of her own father. He spoke words to her that would prove to be prophetic.

"One day God is going to use your voice for a special purpose." Lorna Dueck's father tried to console his broken-hearted 11-year-old daughter as she sobbed about an insult she had received that day at school. It was about her voice, which was so deep that she was teased because she sounded like a boy. She remembers to this day her father's encouraging words and affirms, "I mark these words as the start of my call." On another occasion, during a meaningful prayer time at a women's meeting, a leader spoke very similar words: "God wants to use your tongue for a very special purpose." The leader then prayed a blessing over that purpose. Lorna says, "This prayer time resurfaces as I evaluate my calling."

As life continued, Lorna went into broadcasting and journalism, in a purely secular work environment. "I began pitching 'faith' stories to local newspapers and major radio stations," she recalls, "and as a result was invited to speak in many churches."

One morning, as she read her favourite newspaper, she realized that there was never any Christian voice in the paper. In her devotions that day, Lorna prayed, "Lord, let me impact the media for you!" This was a key prayer, she recalls. "It was a start to watching God put an *external calling* around what I was feeling *internally.*"

God quickly began to confirm her call through invitations from Christian communications, including an offer from a Canadian live TV show, *100 Huntley Street.* Within 24 days of the job offer, she found herself on daily TV with a national audience. Lorna admits that, like Gideon with his fleece, she needed many external reminders that it was God and not herself calling her into ministry.

Lorna's primary calling is to bring people to faith, and the media is her means of fulfilling this call. Her call is to voice her Christian convictions in the secular arena, in a clear, reasoned and informed manner. "God has entrusted me with this ministry...and it's a trust to be guarded." Today Lorna continues to fulfill her call, hosting a Canadian nationwide talk show—*Listen Up!* The prophetic words spoken to her as a child lingered in her heart, and when the time was right, she walked right into her crystal-clear calling.

WALKING THROUGH GOD'S OPEN DOORS

Does passionate leadership apply only to those whom God calls into a position of public ministry? Absolutely not. People who have chosen other careers can also experience the joy and passion of fulfilling a specific call of God in their lives as they walk through the doors God opens for them.

I have a friend, a laywoman, who has exhibited an amazing call of God throughout all the years I have known her. If I could use only one word to describe her, it would have to be *faithful*. But one word is not enough—she is a woman of prayer, an encourager, a mentor, an outstanding Bible teacher and a true friend.

Ida Nelder and her late husband were encouragers and wise counsellors to every pastor who ever led their church. Theirs was a calling to support and pray for the leaders who served their congregation. They were loyal, co-operative and true. But there is more.

Ida has always been a student of the Word and for almost 20 years taught the adult Bible class in her church. The classroom was always packed. Young adults and old crowded in to hear the practical wisdom this woman shared from the Word of God. It was always fresh, and her applications related to their everyday lives. A wise teacher with a good sense of humour, she used illustrations to make the truths come alive. Her love and zeal for the Word of God inspired her students, and many followed in her footsteps to become teachers.

Ida's call also encompasses a ministry of prayer, and although she is now in her 80s, she still attends a weekly intercessory prayer meeting that she led for 43 years. Through the years, she often tried to turn it over to someone younger, but the group would not let her go. She is a mentor to many young women who have come into the group and committed their lives to Christ. It is a joy- and faith-filled group that experiences miraculous answers to prayer.

Her passionate call goes beyond teaching and prayer, and another of her gifts is mentoring. Even in her advanced years, college students beat a path to her door to ask for counsel and prayer regarding major decisions in their lives. Young couples with children love to be around her—to them she is "Grandma." It can truly be said of Ida, "She speaks with wisdom, and faithful instruction is on her tongue" (Proverbs 31:26).

How did Ida receive her call to such a rewarding and fulfilling life? She developed a healthy spiritual life of prayer and study of the Word. She was faithful and obedient to the precepts of God's Word and walked through the open doors God set before her.

God's call to passionate leadership is for all who are open to hearing his voice and willing to walk through the open doors he sets before them.

BIBLICAL EXAMPLES

Scripture is full of amazing stories of how God called his servants into leadership in biblical times. In the New Testament alone, think of how he called a bunch of fishermen, a tax collector and a physician. And how about his call to the greatest persecutor of the church to become the greatest apostle? And that's only a few! The Old Testament overflows with incredible narrative as the history of God's people unfolds, directed by men and women chosen and called by God. These passionate leaders heard the call and obeyed it, fulfilling not only God's purposes for them as individuals, but also, even more important, his purposes for his chosen people, Israel.

A STRANGE CALL

He was 75 years of age when he heard God's call, and it was a strange call indeed. The Lord said, "Leave your country, your people and your father's household and go to the land I will show you" (Genesis 12:1). Now Abram was well settled in Haran with his father and his family. He was rich in flocks and herds, with many servants, when God made his strange pronouncement. Leave everything? Go without knowing where? No details? Just "Pack up, and I'll lead you as you go along."

The Lord gave him a promise of how he would be blessed, although it was incomprehensible to Abram at the time. A great nation? A great name? A great blessing to all people? How could this be? But Abram knew it was the Lord, for he spoke directly to him. He felt the authority and passion of God in those words and did not hesitate. His faith and passion carried him forward, leading his whole family and entourage in complete obedience. In all his years of wandering through strange lands, he never doubted his call, and at every stopping place, as God led him, he built an altar to the Lord, remembering God's promises.

Have you experienced times in your life when you felt that an inner leading seemed to be a strange call? It was something out of the ordinary. At times like this, the key is to wait on God—to seek him and his guidance through his Word and prayer, and also through the wisdom of trusted friends. Like Abram, wait for God's promise and his clear voice.

A SURPRISING CALL

Sometimes the Lord calls us in a most surprising way. For Abram, the Lord actually appeared to him and spoke directly. It was totally different for Moses. He had always been aware of God's hand upon him since birth, but he had never experienced a distinct, face-to-face encounter with God. After a huge error in judgment, a total lack of self-control and the disclosure of a deceitful character, Moses fled from Egypt, settling far away in the land of Midian. For 40 years, he worked as a shepherd for his father-in-law, tending sheep in the desert. Finally, when Moses was 80 years of age, God knew he was ready for a divine summons, the call that would lead him into fulfilling the purpose for which he was born.

In that lonely and deserted place, surrounded by dull, grazing sheep and dry, dusty shrubs, Moses received a surprising call. It was dramatic. It was miraculous. It was passionate. God, speaking to Moses from a burning bush that was not consumed, told him exactly what he wanted him to do and how to do it. His call was undeniable. Moses was the only one there, and besides, God called him by name.

Unlike Abram, Moses argued with God, trying to persuade him to send someone else to deliver the children of Israel out of Egypt. He was filled with fear and used every excuse he could think of: "I have no credibility in Egypt." "I'm not eloquent of speech." "They'll never believe you sent me!" (See Exodus 3.) But God prevailed. Although Moses was less than passionate about God's call to him in the beginning, it was not long until Moses, with God's perseverance and promise of miraculous help, became one of the most passionate leaders in the history of the children of Israel.

I have witnessed through the years how God calls women to amazing positions they would never have dreamed of for themselves. Their first response is "I could never do that—it's beyond my sphere of experience." But God all the while has been training and developing qualities and characteristics in preparation for this surprising call—just like he was doing with Moses for those 40 years in the desert.

GOD-ORDAINED CIRCUMSTANCES

God often uses circumstances to lead his children into a place of discovering and discerning his will for their lives. This is what happened to Esther.

When the search was initiated in Susa to find a new queen for King Xerxes, Esther was one of the young girls taken to the palace to take part in the year-long beauty preparation necessary in order to be considered by the king. Mordecai instructed her not to reveal her Jewish heritage.

Mordecai walked every day before the court of the women's house to watch how Esther was getting along. When Esther was presented to the king, it is recorded that she won his favour and approval more than any of the other young women. In time, the royal crown was placed upon her head and she was proclaimed queen.

Shortly after this, an edict was issued, demanding the death of all the Jews in the land—men, women and children. There was great mourning, weeping and wailing. Many of the Jews, including Mordecai, fasted, putting on sackcloth and ashes. Not knowing anything about this edict, Esther inquired as to why Mordecai was in such grief and sorrow. Mordecai urged her to go before the king and beg for mercy and plead with him for her people. Esther knew that to approach the king uninvited could mean instant death—but she also knew she was the only hope for the Jewish people. The circumstances were critical. The destiny of her people was in her hands. Mordecai's words at that moment rang out with absolute revelation of the purposes of God for this young woman who had risen to the highest position in the palace of King

Xerxes: "Who knows whether you have come to the kingdom for such a time as this?" (Esther 4:14, NKJV).

God did not suddenly appear to Esther. There was no epiphany, no angelic visitation, no burning bush. The call was woven into the fibre of God-ordained circumstances: a God-fearing guardian, a respectful spirit, a rare opportunity and the favour of God—these all prepared the way for God to issue his call to this young woman, who would change the history of the Jewish people. Her call required Esther to take a great risk, and her response demonstrated the passion of her heart and the total commitment to the will and purposes of God: "I will go...and if I perish, I perish!" (Esther 4:16, NKJV). Passionate leadership is absolutely essential for those who desire to minister at the leadership edge, leaving their mark on history, and passionate spiritual leadership always begins with the call of God.

As we have seen in this chapter, God's call comes to each one in a different way. For some, his call is a gradual unfolding of his will; for others, it may be the voice of the Holy Spirit speaking gently but definitively. Some hear his call in a more dramatic way, like Moses at the burning bush, while others have a prophetic word spoken to them that sets their course.

I have spoken to some absolutely dynamic leaders who never understood the call of God and its importance in their lives. As they looked back upon their ministries, they suddenly remember a specific moment, a high spiritual peak when God visited them in a supernatural way. Reflecting on that time and the increased passion for ministry, they realized that their call came at that moment.

REFLECTION

Have you ever taken time to think about your call? How did it come to you? Was anyone else involved?

Take time now to write down all you can remember about your call. Perhaps you could write it in your journal so you can read it often.

How did you prepare for fulfilling this call?

What affirmations did God give you as you waited for him to confirm your call?

VISIONARY

Only those who can see the invisible can do the impossible.
(Unknown)

The key of passion ignites the flame of vision, opening the way to dynamic leadership.

What characteristics distinguish a *good leader* from a *visionary leader*? A good leader is generally well trained, educated and experienced in her sphere of leadership. She has valuable people skills and the ability to build relationships and effectively deal with conflict. A good leader is able to coordinate personnel and maintain a steady flow of activity in order to get the job done. Commitment and faithfulness contribute to her success.

A *visionary leader* possesses the same qualities as a good leader. But there is one major difference, and that is passion. Visionary leaders have a passion in their hearts that cannot be quenched. They are able to see beyond—beyond keeping the ball rolling, beyond maintaining the status quo. They catch a glimpse of *the big picture* and can't wait to move forward.

A few years ago, a friend of mine began to share with me a vision God had put in her heart for a particular ministry. Her vision and passion for what could be done were so strong, she could hardly sleep or eat. It was not too long before the door opened and the vision began to take shape. Her passionate leadership attracted others, and her vision became reality. Her passion was contagious and empowered all those who came alongside to help.

Not long ago, I met with a young woman who was recently appointed to lead a large women's organization. During our meal, she shared enthusiastically how God began to put an exciting vision in her heart at the very time she was appointed to the position. As she described the vision God had shown her, her eyes shone and her face was radiant—passion filled her heart. I could not doubt that she had heard from God. Now as she moves forward, passionately sharing her vision with others, God goes before her, and wonderful things are taking shape, more than she even dreamed.

Some people say a visionary is a dreamer. They discredit dreamers, because they themselves don't have the same forward vision and faith to see the potential that lies before them. A visionary leader possesses the desire and determination to see her dream fulfilled, and she is able to identify steps and actions that must be taken for it to happen.

John Maxwell says, "Vision is everything for a leader. It is utterly indispensable. Why? Because vision leads the leader."

SEEING THROUGH GOD'S EYES

I believe visionaries see through God's eyes. They see past barriers, over hindrances and above obstacles. They have God's viewpoint. Do you remember when Moses and the children of Israel were on the verge of reaching and entering their final destination, the Promised Land?

Moses sent 12 men ahead to spy out the land. Was it rich or poor? How many people were there? Were they weak or strong? Were their cities fortified? After 40 days the spies returned. Ten of them gave their report first. "It truly does flow with milk and honey, just as we heard, and the fruit is like nothing we have seen." Joy filled Moses' heart when he heard these words, but then they added, "However, we cannot go up, because the people are like giants and we are like grasshoppers in their sight and the cities are well fortified." (See Numbers 13:27,28.) These words cast fear and discouragement upon the entire camp of Israel.

But there were two other spies, who saw through God's eyes. They came back with a different report. "Let us go up at once and take possession, for we are well able to overcome it" (Numbers 13:30, NKJV). These men were visionary leaders; they had "a different spirit" in them (Numbers 14:24). When God's time came, it was Joshua and Caleb, visionary leaders, full of passion, who led the Israelites into the Promised Land.

SPECIAL NEEDS OF A VISIONARY

PATIENCE

If you are a visionary leader, *don't move too fast!* Keep the vision in your heart until God says, "It's time!" Do you remember how the Lord directed Habakkuk? He told him to write down his vision. In other words, hang on to it, remember it, keep it in view. He said, "There is still a vision for the appointed time…If it seems to tarry, wait for it; it will surely come" (Habakkuk 2:3, NRSV). Waiting is the difficult part for visionaries. I know from personal experience! When God puts a dream in my heart, it can be so real and strong that it is almost impossible to contain it. Certain it is from God, I cannot wait to share it and start working toward its fulfillment!

I'll never forget when God showed me the possibilities of a neighbourhood Bible study. Most of us were young moms and became acquainted as we took our little ones for walks or went to meet our children coming home from school. Sometimes it was a visit at the clothesline or when our children played together in our yards.

For several months this dream was brewing in my heart. I prayed excitedly that God would show me who would be a partner in hosting this weekly study, and while I prayed I already had someone in mind— a woman with whom I had shared spiritual things before. Being so full of enthusiasm for this vision, I did not wait for God to answer my prayer. I just went ahead and spilled out all my fervour and zeal upon my friend, certain that her eager response would be "Yes, let's start at once!" Well, that is not what she said. My hopes were dashed. My spirit was crushed as she rhymed off all the reasons this group would never prosper. "I don't think it's a good idea at all," she concluded.

I was totally disheartened. I had been sure it was God's idea. When I finally picked myself up and dusted off the disappointment and dejection, I prayed again, asking God where I had gone wrong. His answer: "Don't be afraid to wait. I have a perfect plan, and my timing is just right!" It was only a few weeks later when I felt urged to invite a young mom who had recently moved in across the street from me to drop in for coffee. I had forgotten about the neighbourhood study, but as we visited, I couldn't believe my ears when Diana, who had no church connections at all, said, "You know what I've always wished for—a women's Bible study group." God's plan! God's timing!

From that first group of five women (and many children), it grew and divided many times, with women meeting in homes all throughout our community.

I have to confess that there have been many times throughout my years of leadership when I have had to remind myself of this valuable lesson, and always God proves himself faithful. "If [the vision] seems to tarry, wait for it; it will surely come."

SUPPORT LEADERS

It is vital that a visionary leader surround herself with good support leaders, women and men who know how to make things happen. Why? Because visionaries are not always good with details. While we can see the big picture and understand the major steps that must be taken to reach our goals, sometimes the small details escape us. This is when a strong support leader is indispensable.

Good support leaders, such as executive assistants, executive secretaries or team captains, will see exactly what must be done at this early level and take the steps to make it happen. They are absolutely essential to the visionary leader. Their co-operation will either make or break you—because true vision goes beyond what one person can accomplish. The visionary needs support.

As visionary leaders, we have a responsibility to this support group. First of all, we must convey the vision clearly to them at the right time, expressing confidence and appreciation for the gifts they bring to the table. As the vision unfolds, becoming a reality, we must praise them both personally and publicly, acknowledging their contribution to bringing it to pass. Remember, the vision is not yours in the first place; it came from God. So don't take all the credit!

POSITIVE PEOPLE

A visionary must surround herself with positive people at every level. If you're working with a staff, a committee or a team and there is one negative voice, it will be heard above all the rest. How can you recognize this characteristic? You'll hear these words—or something like them:

"We've never done that before."
"We'll never have enough money for that."
"We like it the way it's been."

So what can a leader do? Pray that God will either change the negative heart, igniting a spark of faith and co-operation, or move the doomsayer on to another position more suitable to his or her personality. She may need to take action and move him or her on, not waiting passively for God to come to her rescue. I like what Jim Collins suggests in his book *Good to Great*: "Move the wrong people off your bus and move the right people on it."

I'll never forget the first time God showed me how quickly he can work in a situation like this. My husband and I had a vision for planting a new church. It had been brewing in our hearts for a few years, and finally we knew it was time to launch our dream. When the first phase of the building was completed, we knew God had blessed the faith and efforts of the little group of people who faithfully worked with us to accomplish these first steps. It wasn't long before we outgrew the first facility and needed to introduce the second phase of our vision.

By this time, of course, the small group had grown, and along with the many different faces came many varieties of personalities and temperaments. One of these new members was given an important portfolio, and only a few months into the year we discovered his totally negative perspective on everything. By his calculations, we would end every year "in the red." Therefore, there could be no further growth or expansion.

My husband and I were confident of the vision God had given us, and we knew we must move forward, so we began to pray. I remember clearly, as if it were yesterday, praying a prayer that was not premeditated: "God, please either change this man's heart or send him a job offer somewhere that he can't resist." Two days later the man knocked on our door. My husband's heart sank, because usually when he visited it was to complain about something. When my husband opened the door, the man handed him an envelope, and I heard him say, "This is my resignation. I've been offered a position in another location, and I just can't turn it down." God came to our rescue. The vision had come to us from God, and he intended it to be fulfilled. As we walk faithfully, humbly and obediently, God will make a way for us. "If [the vision] seems to tarry, wait for it; it will surely come."

PERSEVERANCE

To be a leader is difficult. To be a visionary leader is even more so. There will be times when you will face obstacles and setbacks and major decisions that only you can make. You will encounter struggles and opposition in your organization, church or office, and you'll say to yourself (or your best friend), "I don't need this." You'll ask God, "Am I really in your will? Isn't there something easier I can do?"

Bill Hybels, pastor of Willow Creek Community Church, in Barrington, Illinois, describes a time in his ministry when he experienced opposition regarding growth and expansion of his church. Driving home one afternoon, weighed down with the responsibility of it all, thoughts flooded his mind. "You don't need this. Why don't you quit?" Immediately another voice came, "Remember your call! Don't quit!"

You can discover throughout the Scriptures women and men of God who repeatedly faced challenges of discouragement and wanted to quit. Remember Moses when God gave him the vision of leading the entire nation of Israel out of Egypt? First he faced opposition from Pharaoh and then years of contrariness from disgruntled Israel.

Think about the prophetess Deborah, a leader of Israel at the time when prophets were leading the nation. After 25 years of living under Canaanite rule, she received a clear word from God, a specific vision: "I'm going to deliver my people." He gave her the exact steps that should be taken. Following God's directions, Deborah passed the message on to Barak, the captain of Israel's army, the one God commanded to carry out the vision. Deliverance and victory were assured.

Can you imagine Deborah's dismay when she realized that Barak had no faith, that he was afraid, even though God had given specific directions and the promise of victory? What kind of a support leader was this? No vision. No faith. No trust in God or the leader God had set over him. "If you don't go with me, I won't go," he cowered (Judges 4:8). Deborah did not give up. God gave the vision, he made a promise, and she would go forward! "Very well," Deborah said, "I will go with you. But because of the way you are going about this, the honor will not be yours, for the LORD will hand Sisera [the commander of the Canaanite army] over to a woman" (Judges 4:9).

PRAYER SUPPORT

> I urge, then, first of all, that requests, prayers, intercession and thanksgiving be made for everyone—for…all those in authority [leaders]…This is good, and pleases God our Savior. (1 Timothy 2:1-3)

Leaders need intercessors! They need a group of praying people who believe in them and their ministry and will pray regularly and consistently for them. Because of the many obstacles and pitfalls, temptations and discouragements, the power of intercession in the life of a leader cannot be measured.

Intercessors should be those with whom a leader can share her vision and requests in confidence. Regular communication with them is essential. They will be encouraged as they are updated with specific answers to their prayers.

FRONT-RUNNERS

A visionary leader is a front-runner. She is a dreamer, able to see the big picture and to get God's perspective. She will see the dream through his eyes. She is fired by passion, a passion she infuses into others as she challenges them to move forward with her. Her passion is contagious. A visionary leader soon realizes the importance of patience and perseverance as she waits for God's timing and for her followers to catch her vision. She acknowledges and relies on the power of the intercessors who pray for her and her ministry.

REFLECTION

Has God given you a vision, something you can imagine could truly be possible and yet seems too big for your mind to comprehend?

Have you ever been discouraged, like me, by others with whom you have shared your dream?

Take time now to contemplate your vision in prayer. Ask God to clarify his will and plan—then wait for his leading. Keep the dream in your heart.

As God speaks to you, write your thoughts in a journal. You will discover that he will lead you one step at a time toward making your dream a reality. Remember Habakkuk: "If [the vision] seems to tarry, wait for it; it will surely come."

COMMITTED

Effective ministry can only be evaluated in the long term. It is
a long obedience in the same direction. (Eugene Peterson)

The fire of passion for God is the key that keeps leaders committed
to fulfilling their call.

It was at a church camp about 20 years ago that I first met Susan and
Jim Keddy, just a few days before they left for Hong Kong as missionaries. I was impressed then with their excitement, courage and commitment to this new adventure as they prepared to leave with their two
young sons. As I spoke to Susan it seemed to me that there were some
uncertainties tied to this venture, but she exhibited an unshakable confidence that God was leading them. Through the years I have followed
their journey with interest and marvelled at their depth of commitment.

Just recently I had the opportunity to spend a few hours with Susan
and delve into the fascinating story of their journey. I asked her to
describe how they held on to their unwavering commitment in the face
of the many tests and difficulties they encountered.

Sue explained how 25 years ago, when they began their ministry,
God gave them a challenge that she thinks about constantly to this day.
"It still makes my heart pound and my feet move," she exclaimed.
"When everything turns upside down and my heart is crushed, and I
wonder how I am going to breathe, let alone face tomorrow, God's chal-
lenge turns my face to the sky, and once again I stand, *committed*."

What was God's challenge to this young couple? Simply to obey him in every little thing and his presence would be with them. Obedience—that is the key to their amazing commitment.

"God brought the homeless, the hungry and the broken to our door," says Susan, "and our home truly became his home. First, he took us across the ocean, where a brand new adventure began in a little slum in Rio Mar, Dominican Republic. From there it was to Asia, where for the next 16 years our God overwhelmed us with his faithfulness and his incredible generosity to include us in his plan. We had front row seats to the miraculous and we never did get used to it!

"We had fun. We had difficulties. There were beautiful nights under star-filled skies. There were tearful nights we thought would never end. There was the joy of seeing thousands choose to follow Jesus. There was the agony of watching others refuse. We walked through the good and the bad, thankful we were on the journey together.

"Then, I walked alone.

"The morning Jim passed away with a heart attack, at 46 years of age, I heard once again the challenge of the Lord: Obey me in every little thing, and my presence will be with you."

What did this obedience mean to Susan at that time? It meant a new dedication to commitment. It meant choosing to embrace the sovereignty of God. It meant trusting him for all of her tomorrows as she continued the journey without her life partner. It meant, as Eugene Peterson aptly described it, "a long obedience in the same direction."

COMMITMENT FOR A WOMAN IN LEADERSHIP—WHAT DOES IT MEAN?

Success for a woman in leadership depends on passionate commitment and demands the highest level of dedication and courage, no matter what the obstacles. Commitment means staying the course, continuing the work you have been called to do, whether you see results or not. Paul wrote in Galatians 6:9, "Let us not become weary in doing good, for at the proper time we will reap a harvest."

To be committed means continuing to trust God when it seems he has changed direction on you and you are not sure where you are going. It means to continue on when others have deserted you and to continue whether or not you have the approval of the crowd. The apostle Paul knew what it meant to be abandoned by one of his team. He explained it in his second letter to Timothy (4:10). Evidently, Demas' love for the world surpassed his love for the ministry, and he just took off.

The Lord Jesus also experienced the disappointment of being forsaken. He had carefully chosen 12 disciples and for 3 years poured his life into them, teaching, praying and modelling leadership for them. When things got tough, when it appeared there was danger ahead, one of the chosen decided "I can't go through with this," and what did Judas do? He became a traitor, betraying the one who had loved and called him. His fear, along with his love for money, exceeded his commitment to the Lord.

As you read these words, I'm sure you are thinking of many in whose lives you have invested only to be disappointed when their lack of commitment caused them to toss it all aside.

Commitment means sacrificing time and energy to fulfill obligations and keep promises. It means relinquishing your own desires and submitting in obedience to the call of your heart. While others may be free to spend their time as they will, for a committed leader it is different. Commitment enables a leader to withstand the temptation to quit; it ignores the temptation to give up when things are tough. Commitment costs, but the dividends are of far greater value.

BUILDING BLOCKS OF COMMITMENT

Absolute confidence in the call of God on your life is the first building block of commitment. Every woman contemplating leadership must settle this first with God. This will be your solid foundation when tests and difficulties arise. Commitment will affirm "I'm here in the will of God; I will trust him!"

Our greatest example of commitment, of course, is the Lord Jesus. I've always been struck by this in Luke's Gospel: "As the time approached for him to be taken up to heaven, Jesus resolutely set out for Jerusalem" (Luke 9:51). This is how *The Message* puts it: "When it came close to the time for his Ascension, he gathered up his courage and steeled himself for the journey to Jerusalem." Jesus knew the Father's plan, he knew the cost he must pay to fulfill his purpose in coming to earth, and he was fully committed to do it. Was it easy? No. Was it comfortable? No. Did everyone think "What a hero!"? No. His agonizing prayer in the garden of Gethsemane depicts his anguish and sorrow, but he was committed to fulfilling his purpose.

As leaders, there are times we must be resolute, times we must steel ourselves against opposition and discouragement and draw on the courage that comes from confidence and trust in God. Like the Psalmist, we need to "cry out to God Most High, to God, who fulfills {his purpose} for me" (Psalm 57:2).

The second building block is *tenacity of purpose*. We see this characteristic also in Jesus' life. Distractions will come to cloud the goal and blur the vision. It may be a co-worker or a peer who criticizes the direction that is being charted for an organization—"That's never been done before; we can't afford it; that's far too big a goal."

Sometimes the success of an endeavour will be questioned, so the leader must be careful who she listens to. I learned this lesson very well on one occasion. I was chair of a special committee, working for several months on an important agenda. We had been plowing ground and planting seeds and were beginning to see promising results from our labours when a doomsayer spoke up in one of our meetings. "When are we going to see something happen? We haven't done anything yet." Her words struck like a dagger straight to the heart. For a moment I was speechless. Immediately, another member of the group began to list the steps that had been taken and the wonderful outcomes that we had already seen. The atmosphere of shock gradually changed as one by one other members added their views of our success, and the meeting moved forward unshaken. Being convinced of God's leading in the situation and sharing a strong commitment with the others, I was able to persevere in the face of this opposition.

Perseverance, another building block, means steadfast pursuit in the face of difficulty. It comes from the Greek root word meaning "to remain under." No matter how enormous the challenges or daunting the problems, if a leader is confident in God's call and retains a tenacity of purpose, she will have strength to persevere—to remain under, to survive under, to stay afloat, no matter what comes her way.

36

Clear vision and well-defined goals are essential in building commitment. Have you ever worked with a leader who didn't have a clear vision of where she was going or how she was going to get there? Not only is it hopeless for a follower to be committed to such a leader, it's impossible for the leader herself to stay committed. I have found that when God calls a leader he gives her a clear vision. It may be through prayer, the Word of God, confirmations from trusted mentors or circumstances.

It is a leader's responsibility to find God's direction as well as to seek him in setting appropriate goals. Do you remember when Solomon was appointed king after his father, David? God appeared to him in a dream and said, "Ask for whatever you want me to give you" (1 Kings 3:5). Solomon was aware of the huge responsibility that had been placed upon him and acknowledged his weakness and inability to govern the nation of Israel, so his request was for a wise and understanding heart to lead and to administer justice. God promised to give him what he asked and more. How many women in leadership begin and continue their ministry as Solomon did, seeking and depending on God's wisdom and not relying on their own? What a lesson.

A support group, an inner circle, with whom a leader can share her ideas, is invaluable. They can dream with her, envision her "big picture" and honestly give their affirmation, concerns and advice. This kind of group, or even one individual, is indispensable.

OUTCOMES OF COMMITMENT

Commitment empowers. No matter what a leader may face, whether it is discouragement, disappointment, disaster or personal challenges, commitment will help her keep our eyes on the goal. It will empower her to finish the job, to follow through on expectations others have of her.

Commitment inspires. As I share with many friends in major leadership positions, I recognize their God-given inspiration as they talk about their dreams and visions, and I am inspired with them. I hear in them a willingness to take a risk, to try something new, to launch a new program. Someone once said, "Every great leader should try at least once to walk on water."

When I was invited to become the national leader of women's ministries for a large denomination, I had a dream. It was to bring together leadership from across the whole nation so I could impart to them collectively the sweeping vision God had given me.

Although my executive director thought it was a worthy concept, he reminded me that there were no funds to support such an event. As I shared with him my plan to have the conference pay for itself, I could see in the small grin on his face his disbelief that such a thing could happen.

I had just recently been appointed to the position, so he wasn't aware of what had happened many times in our district as God provided miraculously when we stepped out in faith. "Please trust me," I asked, "and give me just one chance to prove that we can do it." His grin turned into a big smile as he responded and gave his blessing. We expected about 70 top leaders of the nation to attend this three-day conference, but over 350 women from various levels of leadership registered. Of course, the conference more than paid for itself, with much remaining to contribute to ministry and missions. Regarding taking a risk, someone once said, "Jump and the net will appear." I like that.

STUMBLING BLOCKS TO COMMITMENT

Neglect of her devotional life will become a major stumbling block in a leader's path. Inspiration, energy and anointing come from a consistent relationship with God. It is through prayer and God's Word that obstacles such as discouragement, doubt, weariness, negative thoughts and influences and a sense of hopelessness can be dispelled.

I encourage leaders to memorize God's Word and hide it in their hearts so they can recall it at any time. For example, listen to the hope and guidance in these Scriptures:

Trust in the LORD with all your heart, And lean not on your own understanding; In all your ways acknowledge Him, And He shall direct your paths (Proverbs 3:5,6, NKJV).

In the LORD I put my trust (Psalm 11:1, NKJV).

Why are you cast down, O my soul?...Hope in God (Psalm 42:5, NKJV).

Do not be afraid...I am your shield, your exceedingly great reward. (Genesis 15:1, NKJV)

These things I have spoken to you, that in Me you may have peace. In the world you will have tribulation; but be of good cheer, I have overcome the world. (John 16:33, NKJV)

No weapon formed against you shall prosper. (Isaiah 54:17, NKJV)

Come to Me, all you who labor and are heavy laden, and I will give you rest. (Matthew 11:28, NKJV)

But the anointing which you have received from Him abides in you. (1 John 2:27, NKJV)

Someone has said that there is no such thing as an uncommitted leader, and I agree. The example of Susan and Jim Keddy clearly shows how a passionate obedience in every little detail will develop a strong commitment and the resolve to keep going when the way is tough, when the sacrifice is hard and when others don't understand.

Leaders must have the building blocks of faith in God's call, perseverance to stay the course and a tenacity of purpose. Commitment carries with it many rewards—empowerment, inspiration and the joy of fulfillment, as well as God's blessing.

REFLECTION

Has God shown you the key to commitment for your leadership as he did for Susan and Jim? How have you responded?

Can you outline the way you have maintained your commitment in the face of discouragement and difficulty?

Write in your journal examples of how God has helped you stay the course when it would have been easier to quit.

How would you evaluate your daily devotional time with God? What can you do to make it even better?

CONNECTED

Friendship begins when you say, "What—you too? I thought I was the only one." (C.S. Lewis)

Has this ever happened to you? You meet a stranger, and in a short, casual conversation you discover that you have something in common. Suddenly the conversation moves to a heightened level of communication. It can take place in the most ordinary of circumstances—as a guest in the home of a friend, sitting beside someone at a conference or riding on a train or plane. It has happened to me many times, and I have gained some wonderful friends this way.

Passionate leaders know how to build and maintain strong relationships. This is the key for choosing team and staff members who will connect and bond together.

FOUNDATION OF RELATIONSHIP IS FRIENDSHIP

The first step in building a relationship is friendship. A passionate leader, because she realizes the value of strong relationships, must be intentional in choosing and developing friendships of quality. In order to develop an effective team that will make decisions and work closely together in achieving major goals, a foundation of friendship must be built. How does this happen?

ESTABLISHING FRIENDSHIPS

It begins with individuals. A passionate leader must have the ability to connect with people, showing genuine interest in them. This will mean an investment of time that may be difficult because of busy schedules but is absolutely essential. It will mean meeting regularly, one on one, to share experiences, telling how God has worked in our individual lives. It has been said that friendship is a *three-story event*—my story, your story and God's story. Our investment may include giving books or magazines that will contribute to their spiritual growth and development.

Friendship is built on trust and confidentiality. People must feel that you provide a safe place where they are accepted; otherwise they will not be open about their lives. Honesty and humility in a leader are essentials for true friendship to develop. Honesty and a willingness to be vulnerable create trust and respect, and humility builds a bridge to friendship. Aleksandr Solzhenitsyn gave us these wise words: "There can be no friendship without some acknowledgement of equality."

Leaders seeking to build friendships must evaluate their motives. It is possible to invest in people with the selfish thought "What am I going to get out of this?" But a sincere leader will consider "How am I able to invest in the life of my friend?" I recall a time when I was invited to participate in an interesting and challenging ministry. The leaders seemed enthused about engaging me, but something did not feel quite right. I soon discovered a lack of sincerity in their motives. It was not me they actually wanted. I was only the link that would make a desired connection for them. Wrong motive. I have known leaders who used friends to accomplish deeds that were questionable. The friends became innocently involved, manipulated into taking actions that hurt others. Again, the motives were wrong and unChristlike.

BUILDING A TEAM

In addition to discovering and developing new friendships, you may ask, "What about existing friends? Is it wise to consider them when gathering a team together?" I have found it exciting and rewarding to draw a network of leaders around me who have been my friends or associates for several years. These friends are tried and true. I am familiar with their gifts and talents and understand their strengths and weaknesses, and they are aware of mine. I can be assured of their loyalty and willingness to adopt my vision and run with it. But I would encourage a mixture of old and new. This can create several positive situations, for example, the maturity and existing trust and loyalty of the old and the fresh, imaginative creativity of the new.

There are some occasions when a leader must work with a team already chosen and assigned to her. The members may not have even met each other before. This can present many challenges, depending on the personalities and gifts and sometimes the ages and willingness of the members to work together. How can we deal with such a situation and bring a sense of unity and relationship?

From my own experience, I have learned that I must depend on prayer and God's Word for guidance. How can a leader bring together a group of individuals, most of them strangers to each other, and transform them into a caring, bonded team—ready to adopt and follow the vision and mission God has placed on her heart? James gives excellent advice: "If any of you lacks wisdom, he should ask God, who gives generously to all without finding fault, and it will be given to him" (James 1:5). And Paul's words add wise counsel: "Let your conversation be always full of grace" (Colossians 4:6).

It takes time and commitment for a team to bond and establish good relationships. We see this in the example of Jesus as he chose and worked with his disciples. It is fascinating to read the accounts in the four Gospels. Passionate leaders will take a personal interest in the lives of each individual who works with her, endeavouring to encourage and build them up. This will take patience and often forgiveness. She must learn to understand and work with their different personalities. As with Jesus, a passionate leader will truly love people and have a genuine concern for them, listening to what they have to say and always looking for the best in each one. I like John Maxwell's advice in this regard: "Put a ten on everyone's head." I have been shocked to hear leaders say, "I love my work, but I do not like people." I would have to say they are in the wrong profession. To be effective in ministry, we must touch people's hearts first, before we ask for their hands in service.

SPECIAL SKILLS FOR MAINTAINING RELATIONSHIPS

Prayer, both corporate and individual, is the glue that bonds a team together. Regular times for meeting are most effective. A spiritual retreat is also a wonderful experience for a team. Getting away from the normal routine of work will provide opportunities for sharing special needs or concerns and talking about the call of God on each one's life. Genuine respect and appreciation of one another's gifts and abilities will grow, and the result will be unity and a special sense of camaraderie.

Build a relationship of trust. Trust is developed through integrity, proven over time and strengthened when there is genuine friendship between members. It is important to be sensitive to what is going on in the lives of team members. Sometimes the component of friendship is neglected in a leader's eagerness to get the job done.

Paul gives clear guidance for all spiritual leaders:

If...following Christ...has made any difference in your life, if being in a community of the Spirit means anything to you, if you have a heart, if you care—then...Agree with each other, love each other, be deep-spirited friends. Don't push your way to the front...Put yourself aside, and help others get ahead. Don't be obsessed with getting your own advantage. Forget yourselves long enough to lend a helping hand. (Philippians 2:1-4, The Message)

When conflict resolution is necessary, a wise leader will be willing to confront kindly and honestly, speaking the truth in love. When difficulties are confronted and resolved, relationships are strengthened. Wise leaders will respect diversity and differences.

Perseverance and maintaining longevity of relationships are definite skills. Do not be tempted to give up. Carson Pue of Arrow Leadership says, "The world is full of those who tried, but after meeting with difficulty and rejection—they are the ones who quit."

What about that difficult person?

There are those with whom it seems impossible to have a relationship. No matter how hard we try to reconcile, it seems like nothing works. We try reasoning, prayer, patience and love, but nothing seems to help. I experienced such a person early in my ministry and lived under much guilt because I was unable to correct a situation for which I felt responsible. I tried continually to find out if I had done something to offend the woman. I attempted to show kindness to her, but there was nothing I could do to change the situation.

I prayed fervently for God to show me the problem. Finally, the Lord showed me that to try and build a relationship with her was neither corrective nor redemptive. The difficulty had nothing to do with me but rather was of her making. She was a very unhappy woman within herself and was transferring her unhappiness onto me. In allowing her to do this, I was actually being controlled by her. I was finally able to be rid of the guilt and was set free from the psychological bondage.

In *Fool-Proofing Your Life*, Jan Sylvious writes about how to deal with impossible people. She stresses that we must not allow the difficult person to control us and our emotions. We must give that person to God and move on. God wants us to be free. This is vital for Christian women in leadership.

Solomon said, "The wise woman builds her house" (Proverbs 14:1, NKJV). Recently a young leader, beginning the process of pulling together a group of leaders who will be her inner circle, explained how she was going about it. Because she has a very large territory, she has arranged "getting acquainted" evenings in various sections of her region. At these meetings, she is able to connect socially with scores of women. "I'm on the lookout for women with whom I can build friendships and relationships, and I'm asking God to show me who they are." While getting acquainted, she discovers gifts, talents and abilities that will strengthen her team, and she is building her relationships on the foundation of friendship.

Friendship is the foundation of relationship, and there are specific guidelines for building and establishing both. Unfortunately, there are no shortcuts along the way. It takes consistent and sincere effort. It takes time, sacrifice and hard work. It means taking a sincere, personal interest in people; investing in them and contributing to their spiritual lives and leadership development. It takes living above reproach, in humility and integrity. Timothy underlined clear and unmistakable credentials for those who desire to be leaders. One sentence captures it all: "If anyone sets his heart on being an overseer, he...must be above reproach" (1 Timothy 3:1-2).

REFLECTION

As a leader, what steps have you taken to build friendships that could develop into relationships?

If you have experienced a blended team of associates (former acquaintances and new), what dynamics have you encountered in developing unity among them?

What skill of relationship have you practiced and found most effective?

Part Two

CREDIBLE LEADERSHIP

PERSONAL INTEGRITY

God cannot give a large ministry assignment to a small character. (A.B. Simpson)

Credible leadership, the second key to successful leadership, is the personal integrity and authenticity of a leader destined for the leadership edge. Integrity of character is the top priority for Christian women in leadership. Integrity is who we are on the inside. It is our *being,* not our *doing.* Integrity is defined as "wholeness, soundness and uprightness." It comprises honesty, purity and goodness. Our words alone do not demonstrate our integrity; they must be accompanied by a consistent example through our actions and attitudes. Consider the leadership of Jesus. He taught by his life because his life matched his words; his actions verified his authenticity.

Why is character so important in the life of a leader? It is because leadership flows out of character. For a leader to earn trust, she must be authentic.

What are the qualities of good character? The list is long, containing virtues greatly to be desired: honesty, truthfulness, trustworthiness, self-discipline, dependability and a strong work ethic, along with teachability, conscientiousness and perseverance.

BIBLICAL EXAMPLES OF LACK OF INTEGRITY

One does not have to read far in the biblical text to find examples of lack of integrity. Chapter 3 of Genesis opens with the sorrowful story of Eve's disobedience to God's instructions. Eve and Adam were created in the very likeness of God. They were not mere puppets he would control. He gave them a will of their own and anticipated beautiful fellowship with them. His blessings were lavished upon them. They were to enjoy all of the fruit of the garden, with the exception of one tree in the centre that he had forbidden, for their own good.

When Eve encountered temptation through Satan, who came to her in the form of a cunning serpent, she could resist or yield to it. She could obey the command of God or ignore it. Her integrity, self-discipline and trustworthiness were all at stake. Indeed, the personal integrity of all of the following generations was at stake. An immediate decision to do the right thing must be followed. But Eve did not do that. She looked at the luscious fruit, considered how it might taste, contemplated the increase of wisdom she would receive and simply "took some and ate it" (Genesis 3:6).

Eve's lack of integrity that day opened the door to disobedience and rebellion and to lack of self-control and dependability. Other obvious signs of her flawed character were her intentional encouragement to Adam to follow her disobedient example and then her failure to take responsibility for her actions. "The serpent deceived me, and I ate" (Genesis 3:13).

LESSONS FROM EVE'S TRAGIC CHOICE

Leaders must understand God's ongoing purposes to bless and guide their lives. They must discern when temptations are placed in their paths by the enemy and resist him immediately, not giving him a foothold as Eve did. At the moment of her temptation, she forgot God's purposes. She listened. She considered. She yielded, changing the course of her life forever. She opened the floodgate for a deluge of other weaknesses to flow into her life. A leader's behaviour and actions determine her credibility.

When Eve drew away from the grace of God, a bitter root grew up that caused trouble and defiled others (Hebrews 12:15). Eve was a leader. She was the first role model and mentor for women. Unfortunately, her lack of character and integrity not only influenced Adam that day but also impacted all generations following. Because of

Eve, none of us is born with personal integrity. "Surely I was sinful at birth, sinful from the time my mother conceived me" (Psalm 51:5). Paul explained that through the disobedience of one man, many were made sinners (Romans 5:19).

As women in leadership, we must remember that although we inherited a sinful nature from Adam and Eve, God's abundant provision of grace and his gift of righteousness through Jesus Christ can be ours. Peter tells us that God has given us everything we need to live a life of godliness. He explains that through our knowledge of the Word and God's promises, we will be able to resist and put aside the old nature inherited from Adam and Eve and participate in his divine nature (2 Peter 1:3-9).

REBEKAH'S STORY

Moving a little farther ahead, to Genesis 24, we read the story of a beautiful young woman named Rebekah, who God ordained to become the wife of Isaac. After 20 years of marriage, Rebekah gave birth to twins: Esau, the first born, who would rightfully inherit the birthright, and Jacob, the second born. Before their birth, the Lord told Rebekah that these boys would represent two nations, one stronger than the other, and that the older would serve the younger (Genesis 25:23).

When the boys had grown up, Esau came in one day from fields. At that very moment, Jacob was in the tent, busy cooking a savoury stew. No doubt it was for their evening meal. The aroma wafting out of the tent door reached Esau, and he exclaimed, "Quick, let me have some of that red stew! I'm famished!" (Genesis 25:30). It could be that Jacob had always felt jealous of his father's love of Esau, and considered this moment an opportunity. "First sell me your birthright," he said. "Swear to me" (Genesis 25:31-33). And Esau swore an oath.

At that moment, desperate for food, Esau scorned his spiritual birthright and sold it to gratify a temporal discomfort—his birthright for a pot of stew. This experience tells us a great deal about Esau's character. He did not value his spiritual heritage. It was worth less to him than a bowl of stew, soon to be forgotten. Self-discipline was least among his character virtues.

The story about Rebekah and her twin sons does not end there. Half of the Lord's prediction to her about the brothers had already been realized—Jacob had acquired the birthright; his people would be the stronger nation of the two. Now it was near the time of Isaac's death and time for him to give the blessing to his firstborn. Rebekah overheard a conversation between Isaac and Esau about this and immediately invented a devious scheme to trick her husband into giving the coveted blessing to Jacob.

Jacob resisted at first, fearing they might be found out and he would be cursed by his father, rather than blessed. But Rebekah insisted that he follow her plans. With a heart full of deceit, she instructed him step by step, until he went in and stood before his blind and dying father. Although Isaac questioned the voice, saying it sounded like Jacob's, he was convinced it was Esau by the feel of the rough skin on his hands and neck, which Rebekah had covered with goatskins to make them feel like Esau's. She had also given Jacob some of Esau's clothes to wear, so that when he drew near to Isaac and kissed him, Isaac caught the smell of Esau, and immediately he blessed him.

> Ah, the smell of my son is like the smell of a field that the LORD has blessed. May God give you of heaven's dew And of earth's richness—an abundance of grain and new wine. May nations serve you and peoples bow down to you. Be lord over your brothers, and may the sons of your mother bow down to you. May those who curse you be cursed and those who bless you be blessed. (Genesis 27:27-29)

Rebekah, the beautiful wife chosen for Isaac, a matriarch in Israel's history, had allowed jealousy and envy for her younger son to fill her heart, and eventually she became involved in a calculated deception. The character of uprightness, honesty and integrity had been left far behind. Why did she do this? God had given a promise regarding Jacob. Could she not trust him to bring it to pass? She evidently felt she should help God along and so took things into her own hands.

Think of the ramifications of her dishonesty and deception. A break in trust between her husband and her; a broken relationship between Esau and his mother; bitter anger, hatred and fear between the brothers;

many years of separation of family members. If you stand back and take a panoramic view of this particular family, you may wonder, like me, why this mother did not recognize the trait of deception in her own life as well as in her second-born son and work and pray with him when he was young, seeking to teach him by example the way of honesty and integrity. Jealousy, dishonesty and deception removed all credibility and trustworthiness from the lives of Rebekah and Jacob. It was many years later when God worked in the life of Jacob and restored his relationships with his brother and with his God.

Again, in the New Testament, we meet people whose actions betrayed their lack of integrity. Sapphira and Ananias were part of the fledgling New Testament church right after the outpouring of the Holy Spirit. The disciples were teaching and preaching with great power, and many miracles were taking place. The believers were of one heart and mind, and love and generosity overflowed, to the point that each one shared his or her resources with the others. They would sell their lands or houses and bring the money from the sales to the apostles to be distributed according to the needs (Acts 4:32-35).

Sapphira and Ananias wanted to be part of this generous ministry and discussed together how they would do it. They decided to sell a piece of land they owned, but as they calculated how much they would make on this property, they decided to give only a certain portion to the apostles and keep the rest for themselves. "No one will need to know the difference," they agreed, and they lied that they had given it all (see Acts 5:1-11). When the money was brought to Peter, he immediately recognized that this couple was not being truthful and said, "You have not lied to men but to God" (Acts 5:4). Once again, the enemy's temptation to deceive led to the sin of lying, and Sapphira's and Ananias' integrity was lost. Disastrous consequences followed.

Sometimes we are tempted to categorize lies—big lies or little lies, black lies or white, lies of convenience or lies for saving face. But God does not classify them. Here are some pronouncements from his Word:

The LORD hates…a lying tongue. (Proverbs 6:16-17)

The LORD detests lying lips. (Proverbs 12:22)

Let the lying lips be put to silence. (Psalm 31:18, NKJV)

No wonder David prayed, "Remove from me the way of lying" (Psalm 119:29, NKJV) and "Deliver my soul, O LORD, from lying lips And from a deceitful tongue" (Psalm 120:2, NKJV). "Resist the devil," James instructed, "and he will flee from you" (James 4:7, NKJV).

Honesty and integrity are woven together as a tight thread. Christian women in leadership must be committed to truth.

Paul's letter to Titus is clear regarding the integrity of Christian leaders. They must be blameless, morally sound, not pursuing dishonest gain. They must be hospitable, upright and disciplined. In his letter to Timothy, he admonished leaders to live above reproach, to be temperate, self-controlled and not lovers of money. These are all qualities of Christian character.

BIBLICAL AND HISTORICAL EXAMPLES OF INTEGRITY

So far we have highlighted examples of leaders who have seriously lacked integrity, but there are many wonderful examples in Scripture of leaders, both women and men, who exhibited great integrity and left their mark, influencing the world for good.

Mary, the mother of Jesus, and Elizabeth, the mother of John the Baptist, proved their integrity by their humble submission and obedience to the will of God and by their total belief in the miraculous promises God made to them (Luke 1).

Joseph demonstrated his integrity when he resisted the sexual temptations of Potiphar's wife. It was not just one time, but day after day (Genesis 39:1-16), and God rewarded his uprightness, fulfilling the great purpose he had designed for Joseph's life.

The spirit of integrity in a leader displays itself in humility and confidence in God. Joshua exemplified these qualities. Although he was called to follow the greatest leader Israel had known, he possessed the spirit of humility and total dependence on God, and God rewarded him by exalting him in the sight of all Israel. Read Joshua, chapters 1-4.

Leaders do not need to prove when God is leading them; it will be evident by the integrity of their lives.

Consider now a present-day leader of integrity, Jean Vanier, founder and director of L'Arche International, a federation of homes in 34 countries in which people with intellectual disabilities live with assistants, in community. Jean Vanier believes he was called to bear witness to the love of God for every human being as a sacred creation, worthy of finding his or her place in the world, and to God's closeness to the weak and vulnerable. Vanier has devoted himself to living in the L'Arche community home in Trosly, France, and travelling around the world to give direction to those who establish and live in other L'Arche communities.

Over these 40 years, Vanier has become internationally respected for his work and message, shared in his books, in radio and television interviews, and at the many retreats he has led, in L'Arche communities as well as for prisoners and other marginalized groups. His letters, written to members and supporters of L'Arche communities, reveal the mind and heart of one who responded to God's call with trust and who continues to believe that God will lead. In his own words, "I felt as if God prepared the way and I was simply an instrument to pull things together."

Jean Vanier has received many accolades and honours, among them the Companion to the Order of Canada and a nomination for the Nobel Peace Prize. He has met with political and religious leaders around the world, was a friend of Mother Teresa's and has talked and prayed with popes. Yet for all this, his heart's desire is to remain faithful to God's call. His integrity is evident in the transparency with which he shares his sense of total dependency on God as he endeavours both to serve and to lead. With humility of heart, he writes, "Pray that I may know how to live with the poor and never let my heart be closed up in my own comfort, well-being or flattery. Pray for me that Jesus will keep me continually in anguish in front of the poor."

In Bible characters and in the life of Jean Vanier, we find a broad range of traits indicating integrity of character. In Mary and Elizabeth, obedience, humility and submission; in Joseph, uprightness, moral integrity and dependability; in Joshua, humility, teachability, perseverance and confidence in God; in Jean Vanier, humility, servanthood, dependence and total trust in God.

Personal integrity is the foundation of leadership. If honesty is in place, the other virtues will grow and thrive. This is why Peter stressed this so strongly:

> Make every effort to add to your faith goodness; and to goodness, knowledge; and to knowledge, self-control; and to self-control, perseverance; and to perseverance, godliness; and to godliness, brotherly kindness; and to brotherly kindness, love. For if you possess these qualities in increasing measure, they will keep you from being ineffective and unproductive in your knowledge of our Lord Jesus Christ. (2 Peter 1:5-8)

CHECKLIST OF GOOD CHARACTER QUALITIES

Honesty
Integrity
Self-discipline
Teachability
Dependability
Perseverance
Conscientiousness
Strong work ethic

REFLECTION

Consider your current leadership position. How would you be rated according to this list?

Write in your journal examples of times when, with God's help, you exhibited specific positive traits.

Are there certain traits of integrity that you feel are weak in your life? How will you go about strengthening them?

Are you part of an accountability group? If not, ask God to lead you to two or three other women in leadership to whom you can be accountable.

SPIRITUAL INTEGRITY

Successful leadership comes from the overflow of our relationship with God. (Henry Blackaby)

Spiritual credibility in the life of a woman in leadership is a vital key, paving the way on the journey to the leadership edge.

"I want to be just like him." I was a teenager, sitting in a little church in a town in Ontario, waiting to hear the special guest who had come to speak. He was a young man who had met Christ a few months before while he was in the army. It had been a life-changing encounter. Within a short time, God called him into ministry. Released from the army, he began to travel, preaching in small churches and large.

Surrounded by my friends, I could hardly wait to hear him speak. I watched him as we sang. There was a glow about him I had never seen before. His face radiated. "What is this glow?" I wondered.

When he stood to speak, love poured out through his words. It was his love for God and God's love for each one of us. He told us how God had called him. It was dramatic, like the story of Saul's conversion on the road to Damascus, and he glowed with every word he spoke. Little by little, I became aware that the glow upon Jack West's face was the Spirit of God shining through him. It was like the glory that shone on Moses' face when he spent time with God on Mount Sinai when God gave him the ten commandments. Coming down from that mountain, Moses was not aware that his face was radiant, but Aaron and the children of Israel saw it. It was so bright they could not look at him, and Moses had to wear a veil over his face when he spoke to them (see Exodus 34:29-35; 2 Corinthians 3:7).

The meetings in our little church were to continue for one week. I wondered if the same brightness would hover around him each evening. Night after night I waited and watched. The glow continued, and in my heart came a deeper hunger than I had ever known. I knew this man had spent time in prayer with Jesus. As he preached, I realized that his words matched his life. What he said was backed up by how he lived. His spirituality was genuine, authentic. As a young person I prayed, "Oh Lord, I want to be like him. I want to know you in the same way he does. I want my life to reflect your glory." Throughout the following years I met Jack many times, and he was always the same.

Some years later, I met Kay Kerr. She and her husband, Howard, were missionaries in Argentina. When they came home for furloughs, Kay was in great demand as a speaker at women's conferences and retreats. I'll never forget the first time I heard her. There it was—that same glow! Several hundred women sat spellbound as she shared stories of their lives in South America and the miracles God was doing there. Once again, I found my heart yearning for the spirit I sensed in her. "Oh Lord, I want to be like Kay," I prayed. "I want your glory to shine through me."

The Scriptures are full of leaders who possessed such a spirit. God told Moses that Caleb "has a different spirit and follows me wholeheartedly" (Numbers 14:24). Paul wrote to Timothy, reminding him of the sincere faith of his grandmother, Lois, and his mother, Eunice (1 Timothy 1:5). These two women were leaders in their homes, setting godly examples of integrity, one generation after another. Timothy saw their genuine faith and authenticity, and he emulated them—he wanted to be like them.

We read in Acts 16 the story of a successful business woman named Lydia, who worshipped God and whose heart God had touched. Listening to Paul preach one day, she received and obeyed his teachings. Seeing her joyous enthusiasm and commitment, her whole family wanted to follow her example, and they were all baptized.

One of the greatest examples from Scripture of the Spirit of God resting powerfully and visibly upon a leader is that of Stephen. Almost every time his name appears, he is described as a "man full of faith and of the Holy Spirit" (Acts 6:5) or "a man full of God's grace and power, [who] did great wonders and miraculous signs among the people" (Acts 6:8). When he was brought before his religious persecutors, they were not able to stand up against his wisdom or the spirit by which he spoke. His answers to their questions infuriated them. They gnashed their teeth and covered their ears. With radiant faith, he said to them, "Look...I see heaven open and the Son of Man standing at the right hand of God" (Acts 7:56).

This crowd could not bear the powerful presence of God upon Stephen. They rushed at him, dragged him out of the city and stoned him. As he was dying, he knelt down and prayed with a loud voice, "Lord, do not charge them with this sin" (Acts 7:60, NKJV). The glory of the presence of God rested upon him and shone through him, even until his last breath.

These stories prove that God dwells with his leaders in times of great blessing and outpouring of his Spirit as well as in the hours of deepest tribulation. He will bestow upon them the spirit of faith, integrity and power.

ACQUIRING SPIRITUAL INTEGRITY

Integrity is the very foundation of leadership, but unfortunately we are not born with this character trait. Read Psalm 51:5. Because we are all born in sin, we must consciously and continually nurture and develop this characteristic, being disciplined in our commitment. It will mean being honest and true in the smallest details of our lives.

What was it about Kay Kerr and Jack West that was so compelling? It was not their own personal charisma that drew me to them, although they were both very gracious and kind. It was more than that. It was the Spirit of Jesus in them that drew my heart. I knew they spent time with God in prayer and studying the Scriptures. They knew him in a deeply spiritual way. It was evident in their lives and visible on their countenances. What about Stephen? It was not a natural resilience or bravery that enabled him to pray for those who were stoning him. He had a close relationship with God and was full of faith and of God's power.

Is this kind of extraordinary manifestation of the presence of God given to only a few? Listen to King David when he spoke for all of us in Psalm 51: "Behold, You [God] desire truth in the inward parts, And in the hidden part You will make me to know wisdom" (v. 6, NKJV). Again, in Psalm 86 he prayed, "Teach me Your way, O LORD; I will walk in Your truth; Unite my heart to fear Your name" (v. 11, NKJV). God intends that leaders will be spiritually authentic, walking in truth, united in body, mind and spirit. He emphasizes that he, himself, will teach us. I believe that the leaders we have discussed discovered the secret of walking in truth and being taught of God.

HOW IS SPIRITUAL CREDIBILITY DEVELOPED?

The most important ingredient in building a leader's spiritual credibility is prayer, speaking to God and listening to him as he speaks to us. A woman who has a vibrant prayer life will not need to inform her followers; they will automatically see his glory reflected in her. They will notice the difference in her life. She will not lead by her own influence or power but with the authority of God.

Jesus gave an example of this kind of leadership when he defended his credibility before the Pharisees. "I do nothing of Myself; but as My Father taught Me, I speak these things...I always do those things that please Him" (John 8:28,29, NKJV). Jesus spent much time in close communion with his Father.

Prayer and study of the Word are two disciplines that make up the lifeline for a woman in leadership. Jeremiah treasured the Word of God. "When your words came, I ate them; they were my joy and my heart's delight" (Jeremiah 15:16). David passionately declared, "O, how I love your law! I meditate on it all day long" (Psalm 119:97). This is the kind of hunger God is looking for in the development of a credible spiritual leader.

Paul gave Timothy wise counsel that applies to every Christian woman in leadership. "Devote yourself and diligently pursue the teaching, reading and preaching of the Word. Don't strive or argue about words that don't matter. Instead, study God's Word diligently, so you will have the authority to speak. If you do this, you will be prepared for any work God calls you to do" (see 2 Timothy 2:14-16,21). Systematic and disciplined study of the Word of God, as well as personal devotional times of worship and prayer, will determine the spiritual effectiveness of a woman's work and ministry.

Twice Paul reminded Timothy that his gift of ministry was given to him by God and he should not treat it lightly. "Do not neglect your gift, which was given you through a prophetic message" (1 Timothy 4:14). "Fan into flame the gift of God, which is in you through the laying on of my hands" (2 Timothy 1:6). Leaders are uniquely gifted by God to accomplish specific purposes in their lives. I have known wonderfully gifted women who never developed or used the gifts God gave them. They disregarded his blessings and wondered why their lives seemed unfulfilled. It is not enough to simply acknowledge the gift—it must be fanned as a flame, stirred up and acted upon.

In my first years as a pastor's wife, I tried very hard to fill the role as I thought was expected of me. I soon learned that everyone had a different expectation and I could not possibly satisfy them all. Because it was a relatively new congregation, I served as a youth sponsor, Sunday school teacher, assistant leader of women's ministries, choir director and organist. Over the next ten years (and a variety of ministry positions), God blessed us with four wonderful children, and of course it was my duty to assure that they were all saints and perfect pastor's kids. I became very weary of trying so hard to do everything right. I dutifully prayed and read my Bible, but somehow nothing changed for me.

Then one spring my husband and I were invited to a pastors' conference in Chicago. The speakers were excellent. Not only did they speak from their knowledge and intellect, they also taught from their hearts. I felt their compassion and sincerity for the people they ministered to. They were not just trying to please them; they actually loved them! Listening to them as they poured out their hearts, I realized I had been trying to serve God in my own strength and with my own natural ability, and I did not truly love our people as Jesus loved them.

At that conference, standing alone at the end of a session, I asked God to change my heart, to give me a heart like Jesus. There was no earthquake, thunder or lightning at that moment, but I knew in my heart that God had touched me. I felt enveloped in his love as I moved on to the next session.

I did not realize the extent of what God had done in my heart until after we returned home. Once into the schedule of getting the children off to school and organizing my day, I began to have a strong desire to read my Bible. I had always put that off until later in the evening (if I wasn't too tired).

I obeyed the urge, and within a few days, my reading became a morning discipline. I could hardly wait for that hour. My special place was in the family room, sitting on a couch under a window. God's Word became alive to me. No longer was it boring or dutiful. After reading each morning, I found myself spending time in prayer. The hour went by too quickly; the time spent with God became rich. I experienced a new peace and joy, and I soon forgot about trying to please everyone. Friends began to remark, "You are different. What has happened to you?" I can only say it was the power of the Word of God and the time spent in prayer that changed my life forever. He continues to work in me as I seek to fulfill his call to leadership.

This chapter began with stories of people who captivated my heart and imagination about Christian life and leadership by their credible Christianity. Their lives and examples set me on a course to seek to know God as they knew him. I dare to say, most strong leaders can look back and point to role models or mentors who have impacted them in similar ways. Scriptural examples, also, of powerful Christian leaders like Esther, Deborah, Moses and Stephen stimulate us to be leaders of excellence. And above all these, God is calling us to listen to his voice and allow him to shape and develop us into leaders of integrity and authenticity. Over and over he calls us to seek him in prayer, to meditate and study the Word and to be filled with his Spirit, because all successful leadership flows from a vital relationship with God.

REFLECTION

Who were the most encouraging people in your life as you were growing into leadership?

What was it about them that drew you to them?

Was there a particular moment or experience that propelled you forward into ministry or leadership?

Are there particular Scriptures or biblical characters that stand out as guiding lights along your path?

Have you experienced God's powerful authentication of your ministry, which causes people to follow you? Can you describe the journey that led you to this place? Write about it in your journal.

Part Three

INSPIRING LEADERSHIP

MOTIVATION

Anyone desiring to lead at the edge must make good use of the third key—inspiration.

It was my grandson's first year in high school. Always a good student, he also threw himself enthusiastically into every sports activity available. To tell the truth, sports sometimes may have taken priority over the books. Looking back, I realize that he is very much like his father was at his age. Desiring to help Thaddeus get off to a good start in the new academic year, my son offered him a challenge—if he made an average of 85 percent in his first-term report, he would buy him tickets to a Detroit Lions football game. That was all the motivation he needed. "Detroit Lions, here we come!" Bribery? I don't think so. Motivation? Absolutely, and inspiration was the key.

An effective spiritual leader discovers the value of cultivating motivational skills very early in her ministry. While some leaders consider it enough to explain the vision once, set forth the goals and leave the rest up to the team members, a wise leader knows that a vision is not always caught or bought the first time it is heard. It takes repetition—sometimes hearing the message over and over—before it catches fire in the hearts and imaginations of the team. And once the flame is ignited, the momentum must be maintained. Regular motivation is the key.

WHAT IS MOTIVATION?

Motivation is a driving force, propelling forward movement. Motivation stimulates interest, initiates movement, inspires and encourages. In the natural realm, all we have to do is look at the power of steam and electricity that drives large machinery and the jet propulsion that keeps planes in the air. That's motivation.

When it comes to effective spiritual leadership, motivation must be defined in the same strong, compelling words. Our motivation must be a driving force propelling ourselves and those we lead. We must be inspiring, encouraging and full of energy. "Oh," you ask, "where can I get that kind of energy?" If we try to produce it depending on our own resources, we'll quickly run out of steam. Difficult circumstances, unyielding obstacles and impossible people have a way of wearing us down, no matter how strong we think we are. As Christian women in ministry, we must draw on a source greater than ourselves. Our strength must come from God's unfailing Word and his Holy Spirit. This is our jet propulsion.

EXAMPLES FROM SCRIPTURE

What did God say to Joshua when he commanded him to step into Moses' shoes and lead the children of Israel into the Promised Land? His amazing words cancelled every doubt and argument that could enter Joshua's mind. Over and over the word came: "Be strong and courageous...for the LORD your God will be with you" (Joshua 1:1-9).

Throughout Paul's ministry, he was plagued with a physical affliction he described as a "thorn in my flesh" (2 Corinthians 12:7). It distressed him constantly, and he pleaded with God to remove it. Finally, God responded. "My grace is sufficient for you, for my power is made perfect in weakness" (2 Corinthians 12:9). The promise of God's grace and the perfection of God's power working through his weakness was the motivation that propelled Paul through difficulties and pain as he continued his ministry.

Paul moved among the churches he had established, motivating them in their Christian walk. Listen to what he said to the Ephesians: "Be strong in the Lord and in his mighty power" (Ephesians 6:10). Even sitting in a cold, dark prison cell, Paul found inspiration and sustained energy to pen letters to all the churches in Asia Minor. They were letters of hope and encouragement, motivating the Christians to press on and serve the Lord faithfully.

We consider Joshua and Paul to be spiritual giants, but they were ordinary people like you and me. They were called by God to be leaders in their day, just as we have been called in our day. So, let us reflect on the energy and strength they acquired to accomplish such supernatural results: young Joshua, able to motivate and maintain the momentum to move thousands of disgruntled, complaining Israelites out of the wilderness and into the Promised Land, and Paul, motivated to pour out his life for the churches he had established, travelling, writing, and all the while suffering from his chronic weakness and affliction. How did they do it?

The answer is clear. God had spoken to them. They had his promise of strength, support and power. He promised that he would be with them and that his grace would be sufficient, and they believed him. They both prayed faithfully and depended on the Lord. They waited for his directions and obeyed him fully. What was the result? They had power to motivate those under their leadership.

It is no different for you and me. God has called us to lead. We each have a unique ministry to fulfill, and the same strength and power Joshua and Paul had is available to us. Our strength, motivation and wisdom can be found in God's Word, which is "a lamp to [our] feet and a light for [our] path" (Psalm 119:105). If we wait on him, he promises to guide and direct us. Besides his Word, he has given us his Holy Spirit to be our ever-present guide. By his Holy Spirit, we are energized, anointed and supernaturally empowered to motivate those who follow us. Jude affirmed the secret: "But you, dear friends, build yourselves up in your most holy faith and pray in the Holy Spirit" (Jude 1:20).

METHODS OF MOTIVATION

Be motivated yourself. We have already discussed the spiritual disciplines needed to influence and motivate ourselves. Now let's look at a very rich and practical method of motivating others. I call it living in community. What I mean by this is, first of all, be involved with people. Surround yourself with positive, encouraging people, people who are journeying along a similar path of commitment as you and people who believe in you.

Sometimes we do not recognize a negative, depressing person right away, and we wonder why we are so drained of energy when we are with him or her. I remember times when I thought perhaps my moral obligation was to try to uplift them, but I discovered quickly it did not work. I was the one who soon fell into their depressing attitude. I found out that there had been many others before me who had tried and failed at the same task.

Be a reader. Devour good motivational books and biographies of great women and men who have influenced our world. Keep up with current authors who are writing for our culture. Share titles with peers and colleagues. I am usually reading three great books at a time. It is like having individual visits with the authors every day.

Be a lifelong learner. As you are able, schedule time to take courses or attend seminars. It may mean rescheduling your calendar, maybe even a temporary sacrifice of a special hobby, but it will be well worth it.

Believe in yourself. I love the advice of Jim Collins in *Good to Great*: "You must retain faith that you can prevail to greatness (be victorious…gain the mastery) and retain discipline to reach it."

MOTIVATING OTHERS

Communicate the vision. An effective leader must be convinced of where she is going and have a clear vision, as well as the ability to articulate it clearly to her team. A team needs to hear a vision repeated at least three times before they will grasp and understand it. I worked on a team at one time that was made up of dynamic and passionate members. Each one of us was quick to catch the leader's vision and ready to participate to bring it to pass. But each time we met, it seemed like the vision had been changed and we had to adjust to a new plan and strategies. This affected the respect of the team for the leader and for her credibility. The team didn't last long. They found other areas where they could use their energies and expertise. So the vision must be clear, and we must stick to it.

How do you present your vision? I have heard some pretty boring presentations. Sometimes it seemed the presenter was not too excited about it herself, and other times I have heard leaders who sounded totally unconvinced. To effectively convey your vision, you have to be enthusiastic and totally convinced that it will work. A vision also needs some emotional content, the kind of stuff that touches the hearts, the feelings, of your team.

Conduct good staff meetings. These are key to maintaining motivation. Be sure your communication is made with passion in an atmosphere that celebrates successes, large and small.

Encourage. Encouragement will keep motivational levels high in times of success or failure. I think of Jesus and his twelve disciples. Many of them failed or disappointed him at one time or another during the three years they travelled together, but he continued to teach and mentor them, calling them his friends.

Remember Peter—outspoken, bold and arrogant? When Christ explained his coming crucifixion and that they would all abandon him, Peter rebuffed him. "Lord, I am ready to go with you to prison and to death" (Luke 22:33). We know well the story of the crowing rooster that followed Peter's brave words. And Thomas—the doubter? Even though Jesus had told them all that he would rise from the dead on the third day, Thomas did not believe. He insisted, "Unless I see in His hands the print of the nails, and put my finger into the print of the nails, and put my hand into His side, I will not believe" (John 20:25, NKJV). And he didn't.

James and John believed, but they had a different weakness. They were self-seeking, looking for positions of honour. As they knelt before Jesus, their mother entreated him, "Grant that one of these two sons of mine may sit at your right and the other at your left in your kingdom" (Matthew 20:21). And then there was Judas, who betrayed him completely, selling him to the chief priests for 30 pieces of silver (Matthew 26:15).

There were so many times when Jesus could have given up on these 12 men. He could surely find others more suitable. But he continued to encourage and invest in them, believing in them, certain that they would grow and mature and, with the help of the Holy Spirit, become the founders of the Church he was about to establish. Take time to read the four Gospels, looking for how many times and ways Jesus motivated his disciples. Encouragement was the key.

Value each member and her work. A smart leader will pay attention even to small things and will praise efforts as well as successes. There may be times when you have to think hard for positive words to say, but it will be worth the effort. I like to make a list ahead of time of positive things I can say if I am meeting with a team member. Always be generous with praise. And most important of all, express appreciation immediately—waiting a few hours or days will nullify the positive effect of your words.

OBSTACLES TO MOTIVATION

We have considered many positive contributors to motivation. Now let me caution you briefly about some obstacles you need to watch for: indecision about direction and goals; putting members down with negative attitudes and words; criticism; unresolved conflict; deflating egos; and lack of personal interest in each team member. We will be dealing with these issues in depth in later chapters.

Every leader can look back and remember moments when she experienced the driving force of motivation propelling her forward, inspiring her to take a risk. Very often for me, it was a word of Scripture that challenged and inspired me. When I was a child, it was my mother who pressed me forward, reminding me that I was born for great things.

Later, friends and colleagues were my motivation, encouraging and propelling me toward a goal. Reading biographies of women and men who were world-shapers stimulates me to action, and I am strengthened in my resolve to carry on, to go forward, to make a difference in my sphere of influence. The more I learn and grow, the more I can pass on to others.

REFLECTION

What do you think inspires confidence in followers? What does it take to motivate them?

Who have been the strongest motivators in your life? In what way did they encourage and propel you forward?

What have you accomplished because of this encouragement?

As a leader, in what ways do you motivate others?

What happens when you run up against obstacles? Keep a record in your journal, for your own encouragement.

OPTIMISM

> Inspiration unlocks the gate to optimism, that positive quality
> of self-confidence and God-confidence.

"Optimism, optimism! I get tired of your optimism!" My friend Peggy had heard these words and others like them from her pastor husband many times throughout their marriage. Rick was a worrier, and Peggy tried in vain to provide hope and encouragement when he floundered in despair. An optimist, Peggy worked hard to nurture and develop this quality within herself and had discovered its true source. Rick, on the other hand, seemed to be unable to lift himself from the dark clouds of pessimism and gloom. He seemed to feel he had no control over this part of who he was. He refused to believe that he might actually learn to acquire the quality of optimism, a quality so essential for excellent leadership.

WHAT IS OPTIMISM?

Optimism is self-confidence. It is believing in yourself no matter how great the odds are against you. It is the ability to share your enthusiasm with your team, influencing them to press on to succeed with you. Optimists have a positive outlook with no self-imposed limitations. They are described as "no-limit" people. For the optimist, failures become stepping stones to try again.

An optimist also believes in others. She always sees the good in them and encourages them to reach for their greatest potential. She speaks encouragement into their lives, reinforcing her faith in them.

Several years ago, when I was asked to consider the national women's ministry position in my denomination, I carefully considered all the implications. It would mean driving an hour each way every day into our office in Toronto, setting the vision for a national women's ministry, giving leadership to provincial directors, and ministering overseas. There would be lots of administrative responsibility, which did not inspire me, because I saw myself more as a people person. Working with people was my passion, and I could not see myself sitting day after day in a stuffy little office.

It was my family (all optimists) who quickly began to encourage me, affirming my ability to do the job. "Of course you can do it," they all insisted. The executive director who interviewed me stated firmly his belief in me, explaining that I could make the job exactly what I wanted it to be. These people all saw potential in me that I was unaware of and continually reinforced their faith in me. How did it turn out? Those were the happiest, most fulfilling years of my ministry to that point. God used optimists who believed in me to speak encouragement into my life, directing me into the will of God.

What is the source of self-confidence? Effective spiritual leadership doesn't come from trust in our own natural abilities or acquired competencies, although God does use and bless these qualities as we dedicate them to him. First and foremost, our confidence must be firmly rooted in Jesus Christ and the enabling of his Spirit.

Continuous successful leadership does not depend on a person's charismatic personality. It may appear for a time that natural charisma is the strong appeal, and a leader may rise like a shining star. But natural charisma does not have its roots in the true source of confidence, and the star quickly fades.

So what is the true source? How can we develop and enhance the quality of optimism that will move us from being good leaders to excellent, extraordinary leaders? The answer lies in knowing God— really knowing him. It lies in our commitment to studying and applying the principles of God's Word to our everyday lives. We must apply Scripture practically as well as spiritually in order to build a strong foundation on which optimism can flourish. An optimist delights in the Word of God, meditating on it "day and night" (Psalm 1:2). She draws nourishment and strength as her roots go down deep into the soil of God's Word, and she has the assurance that "whatever [she] does prospers" (Psalm 1:3). No wonder she can be optimistic even in the face of difficulty and complexity.

I marvel as I read through the Psalms at how often David begins his songs with lament over his circumstances. He bewails the onslaught of the enemy; he grieves over the betrayal of a friend; he mourns the silence of God, accusing him of forsaking him. But once into the heart of the psalm, David begins to draw strength from the deep inner resources of his soul. He begins to pray, remembering all the mercies of the Lord and his faithfulness to him in the past. This is the true source of optimism: *knowing God, experiencing God and remembering his unfailing love and kindness.*

Optimism is an attitude. Each one of us has the power to choose between a negative or positive attitude. Through difficult circumstances I experienced in my own leadership, I became aware that negative attitudes are actually crippling, emotionally and even physically. We can easily fall into a negative attitude in the area of relationships without even realizing it. Someone may be offended, or there may be a misunderstanding. A positive attitude at that moment is absolutely vital for a leader, because our attitude will dictate our actions. We need not only to choose our attitude but also to control it. We must not allow ourselves to be victims of fluctuating moods.

Choosing and controlling our attitude is an exercise we must practice. It does not come naturally. Even when we feel we have everything under control, we can easily be caught off guard by the enemy. There is wonderful counsel in God's Word that will help us. Paul exhorts us in Philippians 2:5-8, "Your attitude should be the same as that of Christ Jesus." In the most lofty and beautiful language, he describes the utmost humility of Christ.

Eugene Peterson's paraphrase puts it in everyday language. "He [Christ] had equal status with God but didn't think so much of himself that he had to cling to the advantages of that status no matter what. Not at all. When the time came, he set aside the privileges of deity and took on the status of a slave, became human…He didn't claim special privileges" (The Message).

Again, in Ephesians 4:32, Paul encourages us to have an attitude of kindness, compassion and forgiveness to one another, just as Christ has toward us. Kneeling in the privacy of our secret place, praying and seeking God for strength, we determine, "Yes, Lord, I can forgive that co-worker who wronged me" or "I can show kindness to that one who is undeserving." But meeting these people face to face while remembering their shortcomings requires an even greater resolve and determination than we felt in the quiet place of prayer. What we resolved on our knees must now be expressed in our actions. We have a choice to make. What will our attitude be? Optimism is a characteristic of a positive attitude.

Have you experienced the power of David's petition in Psalm 19:14? "May the words of my mouth and the meditation of my heart be pleasing in your sight, O LORD, my Rock and my Redeemer." What a wonderful motto for a leader striving for excellence!

Optimism is influenced by our self-talk. There is an inner dialogue that goes on inside us all the time. You may be saying, "I don't talk to myself," but the truth is, we all do it. How many times do you wake in the morning to such thoughts as "I don't feel like getting up—there's just too much work to do. I'll never get it all done!" Or perhaps you hear, "I don't think my team is supporting me." It may be that the voice inside tells you the new opportunity you are facing is too big for you and you are sure to fail! Dennis Perkins, in his book *Leading at the Edge,* says, "If you are aware of this inner dialogue especially during times of adversity or setback, you will be conscious of the messages you are sending yourself about failure or success. The right messages are energizing, and the wrong ones are deflating."

So how can we control and govern our self-talk? How can we be sure we are sending ourselves the right messages—messages that encourage and build us up, messages that give us hope and the energy to keep going? Once again the answer lies in our knowledge of God and his Word. A powerful declaration is found in Psalm 119:130, "The entrance of your Words gives light" (NKJV), and again in verse 105, "Your Word [is] a lamp to my feet And a light to my path" (NKJV).

Every summer for years, my family has spent the holidays at our cottage on Manitoulin Island in northern Ontario. We love it there. The days are warm and bright. Lake Kagawong is gorgeous, and we enjoy the friends we have made over the years. However, the nights are very dark. There are no streetlights like at home, so to walk along the lake road we use a flashlight. We keep several of them on the fridge right by the door so we can find them easily on our way out. No matter their size or shape, they all give exactly the light we need. Some illumine the path immediately before us, while others beam a far greater distance, showing us the broad expanse ahead of us.

God's Word is like a faithful flashlight. Our way may seem dark, and we may be uncertain about the path. The messages we are sending ourselves may be full of fear and anxiety. The key to controlling this self-talk is to have God's Word hidden in our hearts. The Psalmist knew the secret. He said, "Your word I have hidden in my heart" (Psalm 119:11, NKJV). Peter exhorted us to "prepare your minds for action" (1 Peter 1:13).

Scripture is full of hope, encouragement, direction and peace. It will minister to our needs. As a young woman, I discovered the value of memorizing God's Word and soon realized that meditation was very much a part of memorization. God's Word became alive to me. If I was discouraged, I prayed with David, "Why are you downcast, O my soul? Why so disturbed within me? Put your hope in God, for I will yet praise him, my Savior and my God" (Psalm 42:5,6). When painful circumstances robbed me of my peace, silencing my song, I remembered Paul's words to the Colossians, "Let the peace of Christ rule in your hearts...sing psalms, hymns and spiritual songs with gratitude in your hearts to God" (Colossians 3:15,16).

There were other passages also: "I can do all things through Christ who strengthens me" (Philippians 4:13, NKJV). "Be anxious for nothing, but in everything by prayer and supplication, with thanksgiving, let your requests be made known to God" (Philippians 4:6, NKJV). "No weapon formed against you shall prosper" (Isaiah 54:17, NKJV). "Let us go up at once and take possession, for we are well able to overcome it" (Numbers 13:30, NKJV). "When you pass through the waters, I will be with you; And through the rivers, they shall not overflow you. When you walk through the fire, you shall not be burned...For I am the LORD your God, The Holy One of Israel, your Savior" (Isaiah 43:2,3, NKJV). This is my self-talk. These are the messages I send myself. They fill me with hope and confidence, and although I am only five feet tall, with God's Word bursting forth in my heart I feel ten feet tall.

Do you want to discover the leadership edge? Then cultivate the quality of optimism. Build a strong self-confidence, rooted in an enduring confidence in God and a growing understanding of his Word. Reinforce your belief in others, encouraging them to grow and reach their potential. Choose and control your attitudes so that you live every day with a positive outlook. And listen to your self-talk. Make sure you are sending yourself the right messages to help you reach your goals.

Christian leaders have the responsibility to develop optimism. Whether it is our natural quality or one we must learn, if we desire to lead at the very edge of our potential, we must be women of optimism. "Let the word of Christ dwell in you richly" (Colossians 3:16). "Be transformed by the renewing of your mind" (Romans 12:2).

REFLECTION

Do you consider yourself an optimist? If not, are you willing to try to learn ways in which you can develop this quality?

Check the inner dialogue going on inside of you. What are the messages you are sending yourself? Are they producing hope or fear?

How will you control this inner dialogue? In your journal, write your commitment to change and list Scriptures that will help you.

Consider memorizing passages that will build optimism.

PRESENCE

A leader's self-assurance and confidence are a strong source of energy and power.

The room buzzed with the sound of excited voices. Friends were renewing old acquaintances and greeting new people. I watched with interest as the evening progressed. It was an intimate reception to welcome the newly appointed president of a large national ministry for women. Amidst the sound of coffee cups and chatter, the chair called the women to order. She explained the purpose of the gathering, but it was not until the new president stood before the podium that the din subsided. With her warm smile and first joyous words of greeting, the president gained the attention of the whole room. She seemed to be speaking to each individual personally. In those first few moments, she connected with every woman in that room. My friend, Margaret Gibb, had presence. Her vibrant personality, enthusiasm and passion captured every heart in the room.

In a different setting several months later, I watched as an audience of 2,000 men and women waited quietly for the plenary speaker, a noted pastor and author. Without fanfare, and with an aura of modesty, she approached the podium. Calmly, she scanned the audience and began to speak. From her first word and for the next 45 minutes, there was not a sound or a motion in that auditorium. Barbara Brown Taylor, often called one of America's finest speakers, had built a bridge to that large crowd and held us in the palm of her hand. She was wonderful. She, too, had presence.

What is "presence"? It does not necessarily refer to a certain type of personality. Margaret is energetic and outgoing. Barbara, on the other hand, comes across as conservative and reserved. Their personalities are quite opposite, and yet they both possess an unmistakable presence, an aura of grace, a special ability to command attention and respect from crowds, whether large or small.

Presence includes self-assurance and confidence. It reflects the integrity of the person. A leader with presence knows herself. She is aware of her strengths and weaknesses. She is quick to acknowledge her dependence on God.

The power of personal presence: A leader's personal presence is a strong source of energy and power that she needs to draw upon. When she stands up to teach or preach, when she sits at the head of a board table, when she calls a staff meeting to order, her personal presence, or lack of it, will help determine her success.

GENUINE CHARISMA

We might call presence "genuine charisma." In an earlier chapter, we talked about natural charisma and the fact that we cannot count on it for continuous, effective leadership, because it is built on a leader's own natural talents and personality.

Natural charisma might command attraction for a short time, but because an element of pride often slips in, natural charisma will let us down over the long haul. It exhibits little or no acknowledgment of dependence on God, and the prideful nature of the leader is soon exposed. The once-faithful followers will gravitate to a new leader.

What is different about genuine charisma? The actual word *charisma* derives its meaning from the Greek root word *charism*, which means grace. A leader with genuine charisma is a living expression of God's grace. She recognizes that her gifts and talents have been given to her by God and that her dependence is totally on him.

WOMEN OF INFLUENCE AND SHAPERS OF HISTORY

Recently, I was speaking to a large group of women in a church in our town. The theme was "Women of Influence—Shaping History." There were many professional women present, as well as homemakers and retired women. I was shocked when most of them told me they did not consider themselves leaders in any sense of the word. "Women of Influence and Shapers of History" were celebrities, were they not, well known for their great deeds and generosity, women like Mother Teresa? The women I addressed that evening did not see themselves fitting into that category. I challenged them with the truth that we are all called to influence those around us, shaping the history of their lives by our encouragement, our personal example and our very presence, by our genuine charisma.

THE PRESENCE OF THE HOLY SPIRIT

If you read John's Gospel, you'll understand that Jesus was sent into the world to bear witness to the Father and make him known. We who are Jesus' disciples are to bear witness to him and make him known to the world. I love the way Eugene Peterson puts it in his contemporary translation *The Message*. "The Word became flesh and blood, and moved into the neighborhood. We saw the glory with our own eyes, the one-of-a-kind glory, like Father, like Son, Generous inside and out, true from start to finish" (John 1:14, The Message). And Jesus' own words to his Father: "For those you gave me…my life is on display in them. For I'm no longer going to be visible in the world" (John 17:9-11, The Message).

Jesus was God incarnate in the flesh, so the world could see God and know him. The Word, God, took on a human body in the form of Jesus, and as Peterson expresses it, "moved into the neighborhood." He became one of us.

Those who lived at the time of Jesus' birth and life saw him with their own eyes. They saw his glory, his truth and his kindness. God's "presence" was among them through Jesus. Then, just before he returned to the Father, Jesus prayed for them and for all of us who would believe because of their testimony. He reminded the Father that since he would no longer be visible in the world, his presence must be on display in us. It would be up to Jesus' followers throughout the generations to reveal him to the world, in all his glory, truth and kindness.

Genuine charisma is the living expression of God in each one of us. It is standing before people with the dynamic presence of God flowing through us—when we teach, when we preach and when we carry out the responsibilities of a leader.

MOSES, A MAN WITH PRESENCE

I love the Old Testament story of that great leader who led the children of Israel out of Egypt towards the Promised Land. Moses had been uniquely called and prepared by God for this great deliverance. It was not an easy task. These people were not what you would call saints. They were grumblers, complainers, disloyal and stubborn. There were moments when Moses felt like giving up, but he knew God had called him. Within him was that sense of divine purpose. He knew he was fulfilling a divine destiny.

At a particularly discouraging time, when the people were rebelling, not only against Moses but also against the Lord, Moses cried out, reminding God, "Remember that this nation is your people...If your Presence does not go with us, do not send us up from here" (Exodus 33:12-15). Remember, Moses was a born leader, called and set apart from his birth. He was a trained leader, educated in the courts of Pharaoh. He was a mature leader, ripened in the wilderness of Midian, but in the midst of his greatest work he knew he could not do it without the Presence of God with him. Moses, as all great spiritual leaders like him, needed the power and presence of God.

THE LEADERSHIP EDGE

What is the leadership edge for a woman in spiritual leadership? It is not her natural charisma or her training or education. It is not her years of experience. It is God working through her in the power of the Holy Spirit to accomplish his purposes. This is the source of her energy and power and her dynamic personal presence. Leaders must follow the example of Moses when he prayed, "If your Presence does not go with us, do not send us up from here." To have presence, God's Presence, genuine charisma, the living expression of God's grace—this is the leadership edge.

REFLECTION

I mentioned earlier two leading women in North America who lead with "presence." Can you make a list of others you know who fit this category?

CHAPTER NINE - PRESENCE

As you consider their lives, what is the one common thread pointing to their significance as leaders?

Do you desire to be this kind of leader? What commitment will you make toward this goal?

ENCOURAGEMENT

The applause of a single human being is of great consequence.
(Samuel Johnson)

I have heard it said that encouragement is the twin sister of optimism. They are born of inspiration. Although we looked briefly at the concept of encouragement in an earlier chapter, because of its significance and powerful influence in our lives I want to look at it more deeply.

What does it mean to encourage? It means to strengthen the heart and embolden the spirit. It means to spur on, to affirm, assuring others of our support.

The Scriptures refer often to this wonderful gift of encouragement. Paul included it in Romans 12:6-8 when he described the gifts of the Spirit. "If [your] gift is...encouraging...[then] encourage." Jesus also spoke of encouragement when he talked to his disciples about sending the Holy Spirit to be with them after he went to be with the Father. "You won't be alone," he promised. "I'm going to send you a Counselor, a Comforter, an encourager, a friend, a teacher" (see John 14:16,26; 15:26; 16:7). And certainly, reading Acts we can see how the Holy Spirit became all that Jesus had promised, and more, for his fearful and apprehensive followers who had heard the Great Commission.

Every woman in leadership has felt anxiety and uncertainty when called to a new position or when invited to consider moving into unfamiliar territory. I can attest to this, but there have always been people in my life to encourage me, speaking words of affirmation and belief in me. That is the key—words, positive words, words bestowing hope and inspiring courage.

THE POWER OF WORDS

One of the most important responsibilities of a leader is to discover, strengthen and develop potential leaders. Encouragement is a vital key in this process, and our words, actions and attitudes are our most powerful tools. No wonder Solomon emphatically declared, "Death and life are in the power of the tongue" (Proverbs 18:21, NKJV), and Paul commanded, "Say only what is good and helpful to those you are talking to, and what will give them a blessing" (Ephesians 4:29, TLB). Words of encouragement build confidence and courage, producing hope. Sincere words of commendation spur others on to work even harder to develop the gifts and talents God has placed within them.

I can remember as a child hearing my mother telling my siblings and me, "You were born for great things, so always strive for excellence." These words and many like them were not just spoken once; we heard them over and over. They were imprinted in our memories, and she helped and encouraged us through our growing-up years to make sure her words came true. She always congratulated us on our achievements and hung our many diplomas with pride.

James Robison, who has a global ministry supporting children and families in many developing countries, shares about his difficult childhood and the hopelessness he felt until someone said to him, "I see something in you!" These words changed his life. He began to see himself differently and prayed, "Lord, what do you have for me to do?" Millions around the world have been blessed as a result of those five little words spoken to an ordinary young man.

Words of praise and encouragement come naturally when someone has succeeded or done a job well, but what about in times of failure? These are actually the moments when praise and encouragement are needed most. Unfortunately, our usual response is to evaluate the situation and explain how it could have been done more effectively. We may express our disappointment and even criticize, but let's remember the words in Hebrews 12:12,13: "Therefore, strengthen your feeble arms and weak knees...so that the lame may not be disabled."

I have worked with leaders at every level, and some of the most gifted and talented have been devastated because a project they believed in failed. Many felt like giving up, and it was only generous encouragement and praise for their great effort that kept them going. The writer of Hebrews knew the power of encouragement and wrote to young Christians, urging them to encourage one another daily and to try and outdo each other in being kind and helpful, spurring one another on to love and good deeds (Hebrews 10:24,25).

Paul praised the Thessalonians for being excellent examples to other believers and enthusiastically commended them for their progress in faith, love and patience (2 Thessalonians 1:3,4). To the Philippians he wrote, "Every time I think of you, I thank God for you—and have great confidence in you" (see Philippians 1:3-6). He boasted and bragged about the Corinthians because of their generosity and enthusiasm (2 Corinthians 9:12). Paul was a great example of a leader who continually encouraged those he worked with.

However, if you read about Paul before he became known as the great apostle (Acts 9:26-30), you will discover that he, too, needed an encourager. A few years after his conversion he went to Jerusalem and tried to join the group of disciples, but they were all afraid of him. They knew how he had hated and persecuted the Christians, and they did not trust him. It took Barnabas, *an encourager,* to present him to the apostles, explaining how he had been converted on the road to Damascus and was now boldly preaching salvation through the name of Jesus. Barnabas was an encouragement not only to Paul at that time but also to the apostles, by his words and actions and his attitude toward Paul.

PERSONAL EXAMPLE

Albert Schweitzer said, "Example is not the main thing in influencing others, it is the only thing." People listen to teaching and preaching, they emulate example, and God uses the life as well as the gifts to minister to others. A leader's personal example is a powerful means of encouragement. Her example and authenticity are unique sources of energy and power. I was amazed when attending a conference recently when a woman approached me with a smile of recognition and a warm greeting. I responded, but I did not know who she was. She reminded me about a trio I had trained in our first pastorate and said, "I'm Ruth; don't you remember me?"

Ruth went on to say how she loved coming to our house after school for practice and often to stay for supper. She brought tears to my eyes when she told me it was that period of time in her teen years that settled and secured her Christian faith. "I watched you," she said, "and you were the same at home as you were at church—your Christianity was authentic."

Others are watching a leader's visible actions and behaviour to see how she responds or reacts to challenges and difficulties. If she is in control, they feel in control. Financial pressures and relationship conflicts can weigh heavily upon a leader. Although she may share her deep concerns over these challenges with special prayer partners, it is wise for her to maintain a positive attitude and a spirit of confidence with the rest of her team. Her optimism in the face of difficulty will be the encouragement they need.

CELEBRATION

There is no greater way to spread encouragement than to celebrate. Nothing can lift people's energy and spirits as high. However, when things are tough and stressful, celebration is generally the last thing on a leader's mind. But if, in these very difficult times, a leader can find joys and victories of any size to celebrate, it will make all the difference. A good imagination will uncover lots of ideas—a birthday, a special weekend, a project launched or a job completed, even though it may not have attained the results expected. Celebration dispels fear and tension and rekindles the spark of creative energy and hope.

LAUGHTER

Laughter and a sense of humour are also invaluable and contribute greatly to encouragement. Through the years, I have worked with and led many leadership teams, both nationally and internationally, and have found when there are times to lighten up and have some fun, there is much more dynamic and spirited input into our deliberations.

I currently work with a national leadership team of six strong leaders. We have unity, oneness of heart and amazing creativity as we strategize for each new year. I attribute this to the joy we feel when we're together. It is like a celebration every time. We have lots of prayer as well as laughter as we set the course for the future.

I have also attended team meetings when there seemed to be no room for joy and laughter but rather tension and disunity. I noticed a frequent turnover of people and a lack of interest and commitment on the team.

So, what are the secrets of encouragement? What can leaders do to maximize this wonderful gift of inspiring others? Use words that scatter hope, and be generous with praise and affirmation. Envision God's blessings upon others, and constantly express your confidence and belief in them. Be sure that your actions and attitudes consistently contribute to the good of others.

Remember the importance of personal example, and evaluate your own. Ask yourself, "Do people want to emulate me?" Lighten up, have fun and take every opportunity to celebrate.

REFLECTION

What are the most encouraging words you have heard in your life? Who spoke them?

How did encouragement affect major decisions you have made?

How often do you have the privilege of inspiring leaders, and how do you do it? What actions have you taken to encourage them?

Are you aware of negative attitudes you might have toward others? Describe them and consider how you can change negative attitudes into positive.

What are some ways you, as a leader, can lighten things up and have some fun, dispelling tension and stress in a team?

Part Four
COURAGEOUS LEADERSHIP

PERSEVERANCE

> So that I may finish my race with joy, and the ministry which I
> received from the Lord Jesus. (Acts 20:24, NKJV)

The fourth key, the key of courageous leadership, provides strength for every leader pursuing the often rugged path to the leadership edge.

Congratulations! You have just been promoted to a new position. Everyone is crowding around you with good wishes, compliments and vigorous pats on the back. Expectations run high—your own and others'. The atmosphere is charged. It is a day of celebration, and with the momentum of enthusiasm and support, success will certainly be inevitable. Your journey of leadership is bound to be smooth.

However, anyone who has been in leadership for any length of time realizes that once the fanfare is over and you have set into the work at hand, your position of leadership takes on its new character, that of servanthood. And it does not promise smooth or straight roads.

As God begins to enlarge the vision and the leader sets new goals in place, she is bound to meet with obstacles and roadblocks. Paul gave a wise mandate to the Corinthians: "Therefore, my dear brothers, stand firm. Let nothing move you. Always give yourselves fully to the work of the Lord, because you know that your labor in the Lord is not in vain" (1 Corinthians 15:58).

We discussed the importance of perseverance and endurance in Chapter 2 as it relates to the ongoing relationships of visionary leaders.

In this chapter, I want to consider these qualities in regard to God's call and his bewildering delays in opening doors that will bring fulfillment. And I want to look at the question, "How can one become a leader who lasts?" According to Webster, *endurance* is "the ability to withstand prolonged strain."

THE SOURCE OF THIS SUSTAINING POWER

The source of this power comes from an unshakable confidence that God has placed you in your position. It may not necessarily be one of your own choosing, and you may even feel inadequate for such a calling. But deep inside there is the strong conviction that you are serving by God's appointment. Giving up cannot enter the equation.

One woman in the Bible was given a responsibility that proved to be critically significant in the history of a whole nation. Her name was Jochebed. She and her husband, Amram, were slaves in Egypt during the time when Pharaoh was becoming alarmed at the growing numbers and strength of the Israelite nation. What could he do to hinder and demoralize their spirit? Calling his people together, Pharaoh said, "The Israelites have become much too numerous for us...we must deal shrewdly with them or they will become even more numerous and, if war breaks out, will join our enemies, fight against us and leave the country" (Exodus 1:9,10). So he introduced shrewd strategies against them, oppressing and afflicting them with unreasonable demands for their work. But the more they afflicted them, the more they multiplied and grew, and the Egyptians became even more terrified of them. So Pharaoh came up with a more evil and wicked scheme. "Every son who is born you shall cast into the river" (Exodus 1:22, NKJV).

Jochebed was already the mother of two children, Miriam and Aaron. She thanked God for her precious little family. However, God had a special plan for Jochebed and Amram—the blueprint was already drawn. God was looking for a woman who was steadfast in her faith in Jehovah and one he could trust to work with him, even if it took enormous courage and endurance. He chose Jochebed, and in this challenging political time, Moses was born. While she carried him in her womb, she prayed. Her mother-heart was in tune with Jehovah, and little by little, seeds of hope and wisdom and a sense of anticipation filled her soul.

When Moses was born, his parents "saw he was a beautiful [goodly] child; and they were not afraid of the king's command" (Hebrews 11:23, NKJV). They hid him as long as possible and after three months, when he could no longer be concealed in their little tent, God gave Jochobed an incredible plan. She would build a tiny ark of bulrushes, lay him in it and place it in the reeds by the Nile River. What a risk she took! This was not the path she would have chosen but with a heart full of trust and a spirit full of courage, she followed God's direction. Read the amazing story in Exodus 2.

In time, Moses was adopted by the Pharoah's daughter and grew up in the courts of Egypt. It was here he received the finest education, including the military skills of the Egyptian armies and leadership proficiency.

How can leaders identify with Jochebed's experience? Her call to bear a son and to present him back to God took fierce courage and unyielding faith. It was not a call of her choosing. Fear and inadequacy for the task must have plagued her. But knowing there was a divine destiny for this child, she made a choice to obey and trust God.

Committed and growing leaders are continuously called to move out of their comfort zones, to make hard choices, even personal sacrifices, and to take risks. To have the strength, perseverance and confidence to respond to this kind of challenge, they must know assuredly that the ministry or service they have been called into is not just a job but a divine summons from God. Each one must be aware that she has a far-reaching potential. Can you look at yourself and say, "Yes—my life can make a difference"?

I am inspired by the words of Aleksandr Solzhenitsyn, who said, "We must realize we have a historical mission." Author Joyce Carol Oates, speaking at a writer's conference, encouraged listeners to "Have faith in what you are doing and in the regional way to reach the universe." Powerful words indeed.

There is a divine destiny for leaders called and led by God. Their work in the overall agenda for this world is historical, even as it was for Jochebed. Many times leaders underestimate the power of their influence because they fail to discern the bigger picture God has in mind. Often, leaders will undervalue their skills and abilities and compare themselves, their ministries and their callings to those of others. We must keep in mind the words of Paul to the Corinthians: "We do not dare to classify or compare ourselves with some who commend themselves. When they measure themselves by themselves...they are not wise" (2 Corinthians 10:12). I believe each one of us has the potential to become a world leader. Again, Solzhenitsyn challenges us that we must "hurry after history to impose a shape on it—as it glides away."

Leaders who last are those who realize God has a purpose in everything that happens to them. Each test and trial along the path is for a specific purpose and lesson. God is working in us constantly, developing and fine-tuning such qualities as wisdom, discernment, recognition of our character strengths and weaknesses, and the understanding of right timing.

Looking back to the days when my husband and I were pastoring, I realize now that many of the difficulties and trials we experienced were allowed by God to shape and strengthen us and prepare us for the greater challenges of leadership that would come. I recall painful relationship problems that seemed irresolvable. There were times of adversity and criticism we could not seem to change, no matter what we said or did. The ancient Roman philosopher Seneca said, "Fire is the test of gold—adversity, of strong women and men." Perseverance, endurance and determination during our times of challenge were the anchors keeping us steadfast when it would have been easier to give up.

Cavett Robert, a motivational and inspirational speaker, said, "If we study the lives of great women and men carefully and unemotionally we find that, invariably, greatness was developed, tested and revealed through the darker periods of their lives. The largest tributary to the River of Greatness is the Stream of Adversity."

Hannah, a well-known woman in Scripture, is another example of endurance, perseverance and the understanding of right timing. Reading her story in 1 Samuel, we discover that although Hannah had been married to Elkanah for several years, she had no children. Because in the Hebrew culture this was considered a shame for a woman, and because of her unfulfilled longing to be a mother, she was constantly sorrowful. Add to this the continual provoking of Elkanah's other wife, Peninnah, who taunted her endlessly because she, herself, had been blessed with several children.

Hannah endured the annual treks up to the temple in Shiloh when the whole family would go to worship and make sacrifices to the Lord. Peninnah would take advantage of this special time to provoke and irritate her, so much so that Hannah wept uncontrollably and could not eat.

One year, after the sacrifices were made, Hannah slipped away into the temple by herself. Kneeling at the altar, she cried out to God, "O LORD Almighty, if you will only look upon your servant's misery and remember me, and not forget your servant but give her a son, then I will give him to the LORD for all the days of his life." At that time, Eli, the priest, was in the temple, saw her weeping and praying silently, and with great insensitivity misjudged her. "How long will you keep on getting drunk?" he scolded. After she had humbly explained her anguish and grief, Eli was sorry for his words and answered, "Go in peace, and may the God of Israel grant you what you have asked of him" (1 Samuel 1:11-17).

Immediately, faith leapt into her heart. Her countenance changed, and her appetite was restored. No longer would the taunts of Peninnah distress her. She had endured the years of affliction put upon her by this woman, she had persevered in faith and prayer, and now her hope and trust were in God.

In the course of time, Samuel was born. When we look back in history we understand the full significance of Samuel's birth. The story is not a simple tale of a young woman longing and praying for a child. It goes much deeper than that. Years before, the Lord had chosen the tribe of Eli's father to be priests in Israel as long as they continued to walk in righteousness. But Eli failed to discipline and train his sons. We read that they were wicked and evil men and did not listen to the correction of their father (1 Samuel 2:12-17). Because of this, a prophesy came that God was going to end his promise to Eli's tribe, and they would be cut off from the priesthood forever. "I will raise up for myself a faithful priest...[and] establish his house, and he will minister before my anointed one always" (1 Samuel 2:35).

During this time, God was working in the life of Hannah, preparing her to bear the son who would become the faithful priest for the nation of Israel, preparing her heart to dedicate this son to his service. Hannah was growing spiritually and learning many lessons during this waiting period. God was developing the qualities of patience, humility, faith, courage and total dependence on him. So great was her trust and desire to please God that she expressed her willingness to give her son back to God. "I will give him to the LORD for all the days of his life" (1 Samuel 1:11).

God's plan all along was to bless Hannah with a son, but he also had a much larger picture in mind. This special son was to become the new spiritual leader for all the nation of Israel, so the timing had to be right and he had to have a strong moral and upright heritage. As Samuel grew up in the house of the Lord, the Lord was with him, and soon all of Israel recognized him as a prophet of the Lord.

Women in leadership often experience long periods of waiting that seem endless and without reason. They may be confident of God's call and certain about the direction he is leading, but the doors do not open. They wait and wait, asking, "Why does God delay?" If they could see the broader picture as God sees it, they would understand.

Christian women in leadership who desire to make a mark in history and for the kingdom of God must realize that the path God sets before them is not only for their enjoyment and pleasure. God has a much greater plan. To see his purposes fulfilled will require perseverance and endurance during the waiting time. God will make his plan clear at the right time. Hannah, longing for a child, did not realize that God was preparing her in this waiting time to bear the son who would be a prophet and priest to Israel. And Jochebed, weaving that little boat of bulrushes for her baby son, could not grasp the far-reaching results of her courageous obedience—the deliverance of her people, Israel, from 400 years of slavery in Egypt.

Leaders must see and grow beyond their own ideas and desires. They must trust God and take risks, understanding that theirs is a historical mission. Solzhenitsyn, freed from the Gulag (forced labour camp system) in Russia, was driven to write his memoirs and the stories of the millions of prisoners who had suffered and died there. "I do not belong to myself alone," he wrote. "My literary destiny is not just my own." Women in Christian leadership must be aware that their destiny is not theirs alone.

Leaders must be conscious of the reality of God's right timing. In his divine purpose, his delays are his designs. It was true of Jesus' birth. Paul wrote in Galatians 4:4, "When the fullness of the time had come, God sent forth His Son, born of a woman." It was not too early and not too late. It was perfect according to God's calendar of events. No matter how long the wait or how confusing the situation may seem, perseverance and endurance—with patience, prayer and preparation—are needed for every woman in leadership who desires God's very best. She must remember always that God moves in the fullness of time.

REFLECTION

Have you ever been in a waiting period when you wondered why God was not moving to open a door? You felt certain of God's call but confused by delays and interruptions?

Do you see a parallel to the experiences of Jochebed and Hannah?

What were the lessons you learned at that time?

How would you describe the sense of destiny in your leadership?

How will you prepare to be a part of God's "greater" plans?

Pray and ask God to reveal his purposes for you. Write in your journal steps you will take to move into this new awareness.

KEEPING THE FOCUS

> Only you be strong and very courageous, that you may do according to all the law which Moses My servant commanded you. Turn not from it to the right hand or to the left, that you may prosper wherever you go. (Joshua 1:7, AMP)

Eric Liddell, born of missionary parents in China, lived a life inspired. His story, captured in the movie *Chariots of Fire*, thrilled and ignited the imaginations of thousands. He became known as "the fastest runner in Scotland." His superb example upheld the Olympic motto, "Swifter, Higher, Stronger," and although he was an outstanding athlete, he was described as entirely without vanity.

Liddell's dream was to become a runner. He set his goals, focused his attention, and, one after another, he won every race, first in his beloved Scotland and then on to the Olympics in Paris. How did he accomplish his outstanding achievements? Self-discipline, determination and commitment. He looked neither to the right nor to the left, but straight ahead. You could see his determination as he ran, shoulders back, head tilted, mouth wide open. It appeared almost as if he was looking into the sky. He often explained that he could feel God's pleasure as he ran. No wonder he was swifter, higher and stronger.

Cindy Klassen, Canada's speed-skating sweetheart and gold-medalist in the 2006 Winter Olympics, was the winner of five other medals in the same year. In explaining her success, she described in an interview with

Karen Stiller, editor of *Women Alive* magazine, the rigorous and disciplined training and practice, beginning very early in each season, as well as the importance of watching other championship games and competitions. These helped her understand where she needed to improve and what areas of training she needed to focus on. I'm reminded of Paul's words, "Let us throw off everything that hinders and the sin that so easily entangles, and let us run with perseverance the race marked out for us" (Hebrews 12:1).

Klassen tells of the sacrifices necessary during training, like giving up enjoyable activities and even time with friends in order to keep her focus. Self-discipline—this was the key to her success. Self-discipline is described as mental and moral training, the bringing of ourselves under control. We may want to do other things with our time, but this kind of discipline helps us to stay the course, to keep the focus.

Paul is a shining example. He wrote in 2 Timothy 4:7, "I have fought the good fight, I have finished the race, I have kept the faith." Confident that he had won the gold, he continued, "There is in store for me the crown of righteousness, which the Lord, the righteous Judge, will award to me on that day" (2 Timothy 4:8).

When asked by Karen Stiller how she felt during the race that won her the gold medal, Klassen replied, "I felt it was going to be the best race in my life. I knew it would be great; I could just feel it." When it was announced that she was the winner, her first thought was how grateful she was to God for the gift he has given her and for the best coach and supportive family, who helped her to keep her focus clear and her commitment strong.

As leaders, most of us set out with a clear focus. With excitement and enthusiasm we set our goals and take off with a running start. But often, all too soon, we find ourselves sidetracked, interrupted unexpectedly by distractions. We need to identify these potential hindrances so we can be alert to their ability to derail us.

RECOGNIZING THE CULPRITS

Neglecting to make and keep our goal a priority will distract us, taking us off course. Legitimate things will crowd their way into our attention, and we are tempted to take care of them immediately, setting our main focus aside even though we know these other things are less important. For example, I have set aside mornings for writing, but because I am a social person and love meeting and talking to friends, I am often tempted to check my email early in the morning. I have learned that by the time I have read and answered my messages, I have lost a good chunk of writing time. My daughter gave me an excellent tip for guarding my time: "Don't open your emails first thing in the morning. Save them for the afternoon. Early morning is when your mind is fresh and your creative energy is strong. Take advantage of that time for writing, then tackle the emails and other administrative details in the afternoon." Good advice.

Leaders often receive invitations to speak or requests to sit on committees or boards. These may be legitimate opportunities and appear very interesting, but will they contribute to the main focus of the leader, or will they distract her from it? A leader must learn to say "No," even to good opportunities that come along. There are times when she must postpone less important meetings. It may be necessary at times to put staff on hold when they are clamouring for attention in distracting ways.

So how can a leader become intentional about dealing with distractions? First, she must be serious about reaching goals and willing to make a determined commitment to self-discipline. Secondly, setting up weekly, daily and monthly goals is a practical way to stick with her plan. Thirdly, it is important for a leader to revisit her goals often, evaluating progress. There may be times when an adjustment in her schedule must be made. Remember these words of encouragement: "Keep your eyes on Jesus, who both began and finished this race we're in. Study how he did it. Because he never lost sight of where he was headed—that exhilarating finish in and with God—he could put up with anything along the way: Cross, shame, whatever" (Hebrews 12:2, The Message).

Most leaders have gone through periods of discouragement. These can be caused by a variety of circumstances, for example, extreme physical exhaustion and overwork. Have you ever heard yourself saying, "I'm so weary; I need a rest?" Or "This job is too strenuous; it takes too much energy. I need a break?" At these times, the goal seems too far out of reach, and discouragement overwhelms us. This physical exhaustion is often compounded by spiritual weariness because of the lack of time for prayer and Bible study.

Challenging relationships are the most common roadblocks the enemy uses to interrupt the focus and destroy the self-discipline of a leader. When time and energy are spent trying to understand and repair a broken friendship or association, the key task is set aside and precious time is lost. Attention turns from the primary goal to trying to settle a crisis. The situation is intensified by the emotional and psychological stress that accompanies such a challenge. During these times, a leader must look to the Lord for wisdom. James admonishes us to always ask God for wisdom, because he will give it to us liberally (James 1:5). Paul encourages us not to "fret or have any anxiety about anything, but in every circumstance and in everything, by prayer and petition (definite requests), with thanksgiving, continue to make [our] wants known to God" (Philippians 4:6, AMP).

Paul wrote to the Philippians, "The peace of God, which transcends all understanding, will guard your hearts and your minds in Christ Jesus" (Philippians 4:7). The Psalmist declared, "God is our refuge and strength, an ever-present help in trouble" (Psalm 46:1) and "The LORD Almighty is with us; the God of Jacob is our fortress" (Psalm 46:11).

It is critical to have trusted friends to walk with you through diffi-cult situations, providing insight, encouragement and faith. Throughout my leadership, I have been blessed to have such friends, and it has been my privilege to be that kind of special friend to others. The support of these friends is an invaluable aid to a leader in keeping her focus.

In an earlier chapter, I wrote about difficult people and relationships that are beyond our ability to restore. But there are many times when with a little effort we can resolve a disagreement or a nagging con-tention. Jesus spoke to thousands in his Sermon on the Mount about these problems. "If you are offering your gift at the altar and there remember that your brother has something against you, leave your gift there in front of the altar. First go and be reconciled to your brother; then come and offer your gift" (Matthew 5:23,24).

Depression, often caused by physical or spiritual weariness, can also be a hindrance to keeping your focus on your goal. That is why it is so important for a leader to schedule time for physical rest and relaxation and to be attentive to the spiritual disciplines. When the disciples returned to Jesus after ministering from village to village, Jesus recognized their need to rest: "Come with me by yourselves to a quiet place and get some rest" (Mark 6:31). They needed to be away from the demands and confusion of the crowds. It is no less urgent for leaders today. Much energy is spent in ministering, praying, organizing and all that goes into leadership. A wise leader will take at least one day off during the week. Some recommend scheduling retreat days every few months. A leader must pay attention to her needs for physical and spiritual renewal and wisely plan for these to be met.

We have discussed the many challenges that leaders face as they pursue their dreams and goals, as well as the importance of self-discipline to enable them to stay the course. Athletes such as Eric Liddell and Cindy Klassen are excellent examples. They each had a dream and focused their entire attention and energies to accomplish what they set out to do. It took sacrifice, determination and discipline, and it won them success. Leaders who sincerely desire to fulfill the calling God has placed upon them can learn from these athletes. They can be watchful for the temptations that draw them away from the main goals and be intentional about resisting them. It will take determination to keep the goal a priority, to refuse to make excuses and to guard the discipline of regular physical and spiritual renewal.

"Do you not know that in a race all the runners run, but only one gets the prize? Run in such a way as to get the prize. Everyone who competes in the games goes into strict training" (1 Corinthians 9:24,25). Eugene Peterson puts it this way in *The Message*: "I don't know about you, but I'm running hard for the finish line. I'm giving it everything I've got. No sloppy living for me! I'm staying alert and in top condition. I'm not going to get caught napping, telling everyone else all about it and then missing out myself" (1 Corinthians 9:26,27, The Message).

REFLECTION

In your leadership position, have you established clearly in your mind what your main goal is?

Have you been able to set short-term goals that will help you reach your main goal?

Have you prepared a weekly and monthly schedule that will help you keep on track?

What are the main hindrances or obstacles that interfere with your self-discipline and commitment?

How will you go about controlling these interruptions?

Part Five

NURTURING LEADERSHIP

MENTORING

> Mentoring is a relational experience in which one person
> empowers the other by sharing God-given resources.
> (Paul D. Stanley and J. Robert Clinton)

Nurturing, the fifth key, is one of the most effective ways to open the
way to leading at the edge. Successful leadership happens when one generation nurtures the next.

"Eileen, will you mentor me?" I was sharing an office with a young
executive assistant when she surprised me with this question. I had no
idea that Sandra had been watching me and listening to my conversations during those few months we worked side by side. Sandra was a
Bible college graduate and was working in our office while waiting for
an open door into youth ministry. We set up a time and began to meet
monthly. She was full of questions, and our lunch hours passed very
quickly. I listened, offered suggestions and related some of my own
experiences.

Prayerfully, I shared with her some of the lessons God had taught
me on my ministry journey: to be patient while waiting for open
doors; to take the opportunity for personal evaluation and growth
while waiting; to be faithful in prayer and seek God for guidance; and
how to overcome disappointments and keep on trusting. There was
much more during the several months we spent time together, and our
relationship grew.

My mentoring experience with Sandra is a simple example of what it takes to build a mentoring relationship. While every leader bears the responsibility of personally investing in the lives of new, emerging or developing leaders, I have found that leaders at every level are seeking to be mentored also, by peers or those who are ahead of them on the journey.

FUNDAMENTAL DYNAMICS FOR BUILDING A MENTORING RELATIONSHIP

Paul D. Stanley and J. Robert Clinton, in their book *Connecting*, explain the three dynamics fundamental to the mentoring relationship. The first is *attraction*. This is the starting point. There must be an attraction between the mentor and the mentoree. Generally, this happens because the mentoree perceives the skills and experience, values and commitments of the mentor, along with her wisdom, character and influence. The mentor is attracted because she sees potential in the mentoree and recognizes that she is eager to learn. The mentor welcomes the opportunity to influence an emerging leader.

The second dynamic vital to a mentoring relationship is *responsiveness*. When I met with Sandra, she was eager and willing to learn. Her attitude was responsive and receiving. This receptive spirit made it easy and pleasurable for me as a mentor, and I could see the progress each time we met.

The third dynamic of mentoring is *accountability*. I discovered that I needed to take the initiative in setting the agenda for accountability between Sandra and me. It not only strengthened the relationship when we reviewed and evaluated our progress but also encouraged her to be faithful in following through on applications. This enhanced her empowerment.

TRUE SUCCESS COMES ONLY WHEN EVERY GENERATION CONTINUES TO DEVELOP THE NEXT GENERATION

Every leader bears a responsibility to invest herself in the lives of people within her sphere of influence and particularly those she is specifically appointed to lead.

Simply stated, mentoring is passing to others what we have been given. In looking back, every leader will discover that at least five people in her lifetime have significantly enhanced her development.

Paul D. Stanley and J. Robert Clinton describe many types of mentoring in their book *Connecting*. We will discuss here the most common types and how we can use them for our own development and for empowering and developing others.

ROLE MODELLING

Mentoring can happen incidentally as we live out our lives, and we may not even be aware of it. This is called modelling. In our first church, there was a layman, Alf Cowell, who had a strong influence on my life. I had never met anyone quite like him. A humble man, he was involved in the church and demonstrated a true compassion for people. I soon realized that his compassion came from his vibrant relationship with God. Alf loved God, and he loved people. God's love flowed from his heart to everyone he met. Because of God's Spirit within him, people were drawn to him, and many came to faith in Christ through his witness.

Watching and listening to him created in me a longing to know God as he did and to experience his passion for Christ and others. Alf was not only a spiritual example and role model; he also inspired others to emulate him. He inspired many by his way of life. His influence continues to guide my life today.

A few years ago, I was invited to attend a youth service in Winnipeg. As I sat and listened to the young pastor, I saw myself, I heard my words and I recognized my tone of voice. It was my son teaching the youth that evening. Throughout his teen years, I was sure he was not really listening to me, but that night in Winnipeg I realized that modelling certainly had taken place over the years.

A teacher friend of mine shared an interesting story with me. It happened one blustery, rainy day when her grades 2 and 3 children were having recess inside. They loved to play school even at recess, appointing one child as the teacher to write lessons on the blackboard for the others. All of a sudden, she heard the teacher scolding the children in a loud voice. "You did not do your homework!" Looking up, my friend saw the austere look on the face of the child at the blackboard. She could hardly believe it—was this child modelling her? She realized that day that she was a role model for these children and was not doing very well. The children taught her a valuable lesson.

During my first year of college, there was one subject I dreaded more than any other. The subject was church history, and it was an hour-long class. But when Mrs. Charles Wortman entered the room and began to speak, suddenly the room was electrified as she passionately poured out her knowledge. We were spellbound. That very first lecture was etched in my mind for years. She not only taught facts but also created in us a love and appreciation for knowledge and history. We couldn't wait for her next class.

When I asked a young leader to tell me about mentors who had invested in her life, she responded quickly, "There are two that come immediately to mind." She explained that one of the women was a public figure she had admired from an early age. She had watched her life, how she dealt with problems and struggles, how she endured in the face of difficulties, and how resilient she was in recovering from life's unkind blows. "I wanted to emulate her strong faith and trust in God and her spirit of optimism."

The second mentor she described was a quiet but strong woman. This mentor became a close friend, a confidant and a prayer partner. She was a woman of humility and integrity who spoke volumes into her young life. The influence of both mentors still guides her life.

DIVINE ENCOUNTERS AND DIRECTIONS

God often brings people into our lives who may speak a word of direction or encouragement to us or pose a question at just the right time. In looking back, we realize they were a God-given resource for that specific moment. He also uses us in the same way for the benefit of others. These divine encounters provide momentary opportunities for mentoring.

A colleague of mine, who I meet only occasionally and briefly, said to me recently, "Last year, you said something to me that I never forgot. It has guided me all year as I have passed through deep waters." I had forgotten our conversation, but God used the words of that momentary encounter to speak into his life.

A leader I know has been praying for specific directions for her future. While there are many areas she would be interested in if the doors opened for her, there is one specific idea that has captured her heart. While she was visiting over lunch one day with a casual friend who was unaware of her inner feelings, the friend began to set forth the positive possibilities of the very avenue that is on her heart. My friend took this as a confirmation that she is on the right track. The other woman did not realize that her words may have been prophetic. That was a divine encounter.

HISTORICAL MENTORS

One of the most thrilling mentoring styles is found in the pages of books—stories, autobiographies and biographies of heroes of the past. Stanley and Clinton call these "passive mentors." Reading their stories helps us discover the values and principles, habits and disciplines that made them great. Their influence empowers us even to this day.

Dr. Hudson Taylor, founder of the China Inland Mission and known as the father of modern missions, is one of my favourites. I have read his story over and over, and every time a new zeal and passion is kindled within me to know God with the depth of intimacy and trust he did. His life inspired many, including another favourite of mine—Amy Carmichael.

Although Carmichael was a frail young woman, she heard God say to her, "Go ye…" and she did not hesitate to respond to the call, serving a few years in Japan and then for the remainder of her life in India. Even when a fall in 1948 crippled her and she never walked again, she continued to write and mentor others by her writings.

Carmichael, a single woman, portrayed a life of steadfast endurance in the face of overwhelming obstacles, and the determination to take risks no matter what the cost. She modelled a deep compassion for suffering women and was one of the first to take in women and girl refugees. At great risk to herself and her ministry, she rescued a "temple child" who had been sold into prostitution. She began a mission and then an orphanage. There are four excellent books depicting her history. Her story is life-changing. She is a true mentor.

Other heroes of history are Jim and Elizabeth Elliot, missionaries to Ecuador, where Jim sacrificed his life to win the lost; William Carey, a great missionary evangelist to India; Rees Howells, a Welsh miner, missionary to south Africa, who became an intercessor and opened a Bible college in

Britain to teach the principles of intercession; Mother Teresa; and George Mueller, pastor and founder of an orphanage in Bristol, England, who trusted God implicitly for provision for his entire ministry. You can add to this list heroes you have read about who have mentored you by their lives.

BIBLICAL EXAMPLES

Scripture is rich in examples of mentoring.

When Moses was called by God to go up to Mount Sinai to receive the ten commandments, we read, "Moses set out with Joshua his aide" (Exodus 24:13). It seems that from the time Joshua was young, Moses recognized his potential and began to invest in him, taking him along, providing opportunities for leadership and creating an empowering relationship experience. Just before Moses died, God instructed him to commission Joshua to be his successor. Moses displayed his powerful gift of encouragement, so vital in the mentoring process, when he said to Joshua in the presence of all of Israel, "Be strong and courageous...The LORD himself goes before you and will be with you; he will never leave you nor forsake you. Do not be afraid; do not be discouraged" (Deuteronomy 31:7,8). All of Moses' mentoring through the years culminated in his final proclamation to Joshua, providing him with the strength, courage and empowerment to step into the shoes of this great leader.

I love the fascinating story of mentoring between Elijah and Elisha. It had been a tumultuous time in the history of Israel under the reign of King Ahab and Queen Jezebel, and especially perilous for the prophet Elijah. At this time, the Lord sent Elijah to anoint a new prophet to succeed him. The call was totally surprising and unexpected for the young Elisha. He was not in the school of the prophets, praying, reading, sacrificing. He was a farmer. Elijah found him plowing in the fields with his oxen and servants. He went up to him, threw his cloak around him and moved on. What a strange and unusual call! What did this action mean? Was it a gesture of friendship? Was it an indication that Elijah would take Elisha under his care and be a mentor to him? Was it a sign that Elisha would be clothed with the spirit of Elijah one day?

Immediately Elisha returned to his home, made a feast for his family, said goodbye and followed Elijah. He left his farming behind and went after the prophet of God. They became inseparable, Elisha staying close and watching every miracle, listening to every word of Elijah. Elisha's passionate request of him before he was taken into heaven was "Let me inherit a double portion of your spirit" (2 Kings 2:9). Eugene Peterson puts it this way in *The Message*: "Your life repeated in my life. I want to be a holy man just like you." And God answered his request. Elijah had mentored his successor well, empowering him to carry out the work of a prophet, doing miracles and wonders as he himself had done.

Turning to the New Testament, we find Barnabas, who possessed the gift of encouragement. His name actually means "Son of Encouragement" (Acts 4:36). One of the people he mentored was Paul. After Paul's dramatic conversion on the road to Damascus, he immediately began to teach in the temple there, and the people were astonished and suspicious of him. When he went up to Jerusalem, the disciples there did not receive him either. But Barnabas arrived and spoke on Paul's behalf, explaining how he had met the Lord and was truly a believer and had already been preaching Christ boldly in Damascus (Acts 9:26-28). Barnabas stood up for Paul and opened many doors of ministry for him, another evidence of a good mentor.

As a matter of fact, Paul grew beyond Barnabas in his ministry, and you can read in Acts 13 how he rose as the leader, taking authority to answer questions and preach to the people. There was a shift in roles of the two men, and Barnabas stepped back, realizing that God was developing Paul to his full potential.

Paul became a powerful mentor himself. He used modelling and teaching when mentoring the believers in Corinth. "Therefore I urge you to imitate me" (1 Corinthians 4:16). And again, "Follow my example, as I follow the example of Christ" (1 Corinthians 11:1). He encouraged them to consider him their role model, and he became totally transparent in his relationship with them. "Whatever you have learned or received or heard from me, or seen in me—put it into practice," he told the Philippians (Philippians 4:9). This was Paul's approach to ministry in general, not only to the churches but to individuals as well.

Discernment is important in mentoring. This is the ability to recognize when God is at work in a life, to be spiritually observant and see a situation through God's eyes and to help the mentoree discover what God is up to. This quality is seen clearly in the story of Eli and Samuel

(1 Samuel 3). Eli the priest became a mentor to young Samuel, teaching him by example and lessons the ways of the priesthood.

One evening Samuel heard his name being called. Assuming that it was Eli, the child ran to where Eli was resting. But Eli hadn't called, and he told the boy to go back to bed. Three times the same thing happened, and suddenly Eli knew it was God calling Samuel. In 1 Samuel 3:1, we read, "In those days the word of the LORD was rare," meaning God was not speaking or giving visions to his people. With excitement, Eli told Samuel to go back and if the call came again to answer, "Speak, LORD, for your servant is listening" (1 Samuel 3:9). From that time on, the Lord continued to reveal himself to Samuel, and eventually Samuel was recognized by all Israel as the prophet of the Lord.

Discerning mentors will help mentorees pay attention to the voice and presence of God in everyday circumstances by asking questions or making statements pointing to these discoveries. Keith R. Anderson and Randy D. Reese, in their book *Spiritual Mentoring*, suggest such questions as "Have you noted a pattern of God's movement in your life?" and "What might God want you to hear in the events of your life?" In his book *Under the Unpredictable Plant*, Eugene Peterson encourages us to pay attention to the activity of the Holy Spirit in the routine. He encourages us to ask what the Holy Spirit is doing and saying, in all of our circumstances and to honor the everyday.

OTHER MENTORING TYPES

We have dealt with only a few of the types of mentoring here. Others include discipling, spiritual guidance, spiritual coaching, counselling, sponsoring and peer mentoring. Stanley and Clinton, in their book *Connecting*, also emphasize the necessity of a constellation of mentors, a range of relationships a leader needs over her lifetime. It includes upward mentors, those who have gone farther on their journey than she has; downward mentoring, for those who are following her; and peer-mentors, those walking beside her who are able to mutually edify and encourage her.

MAKING ROOM FOR NEW LEADERS

How can a leader prepare others to step into new opportunities? It is important that she does not consider all members of her team to be followers. She must realize that there are potential leaders among them and provide occasions for them to grow. Delegating work with the authority to carry it out is one of the best ways to enhance leadership skills in others. Of course, this means taking risks, and leaders are often tempted to interfere, but developing leaders must be given permission to fail and support when they do. "Encourage one another daily" (Hebrews 3:13). Sometimes failure is a good teacher, and everyone needs a second chance.

A wise leader gives credit where credit is due, acknowledging success and praising generously. "Let us consider how we may spur one another on toward love and good deeds" (Hebrews 10:24). I have seen leaders take the applause for a job well done when it did not belong to them. This results in resentment and loss of respect for the leader. To truly build up a developing leader, we must take every opportunity to praise her for her accomplishments. If, however, things have not gone as well as expected, a good leader will help her learn from the experience, without criticism and embarrassment.

A leader with confidence in her own strengths and abilities will be able to make room for others. Without confidence, she could feel threatened that if she helps others, they may rise above her and she may lose her own place and position. Insecurity, suspicion and jealousy can prevent the finest leader from making room for others and ultimately destroy her reputation. Weak leaders fight against change for the same reason. In his book *The Twenty-one Irrefutable Laws of Leadership,* John Maxwell writes, "Only secure leaders are able to give power to others."

REFLECTION

Which style of mentoring are you most familiar with?

Consider those who have influenced you in your personal development. Which type of mentoring did they use?

Who have been the historical models in your life? How have they impacted you?

Who are you mentoring at this point in your life? Which type of mentoring are you using?

What leaders took risks to give you the opportunities to develop as a leader?

How are you currently opening doors for others?

How have you encouraged those who failed the first time?

INVESTING IN OTHERS

> People will forget what you said; people will forget what you
> did; but people will never forget how you made them feel.
> (Maya Angelou)

You may wonder as you read this title what the difference is between mentoring and investing in others. Certainly mentoring is a major aspect of investing, but in this chapter I want to look a little more deeply. Are there other practical, everyday ways leaders can intentionally pour themselves into others?

What about the undiscovered leader? Who is noticing her and beginning to instill confidence and inspiration in her, explaining to her that she has gifts and talents that God wants her to cultivate? What about the timid, hesitant emerging leader who is too fearful to step forward and ask for mentoring? Is there anyone to take note of her and cheer her on with generous amounts of reassurance? How about the youth? Is it too soon for leaders to begin pouring their lives into them? In their book *Spiritual Leadership*, Richard and Henry Blackaby stress that any strategy for developing spiritual leaders must take into account emerging leaders currently in their teens. Investing in them will guide and influence their lives.

GIVING YOURSELF AWAY

There are numerous ways to pour yourself into others. If, for example, you want to communicate "I see potential in you, and I want to help you," then share an inspiring book or give a subscription to a magazine that will contribute to spiritual and leadership growth. When I am working with a group or directing a committee or a team, I consider it an investment with great dividends to give each one a book, and always I write an affirmative inscription in it, expressing my sense of the positive future I believe God has in store for him or her.

Personal notes and letters affirming and encouraging people are a great way to give yourself to others. These can be congratulations for a promotion or a job well done, a promise of prayer or an inspiring word of Scripture.

Time is a wonderful gift. Most leaders live busy lives. Our first thought is "How can I add one more thing to my schedule?" But a gift of time to our staff, students or committees, corporately or individually, is a great investment. Take them to lunch or dinner. Build friendships and relationships. Be yourself. Be real. Be vulnerable. Be willing to share your story. Others will be strengthened, encouraged and built up when they realize that you have come through some of the same struggles and difficulties they are experiencing.

During the years that my husband and I pastored, some of the young people in our youth group attended a high school near our home. I can't remember exactly how it started, but I found myself making lunch for several students every Wednesday. I never knew who or how many would come. It was always different. Sometimes they just wanted to talk; other times they had so many questions I could hardly keep up with them. Their questions always led to us having a quick prayer before they returned to school. It wasn't long until these young people wondered if they could meet weekly for an evening Bible study. For several years, 20 or more gathered every Tuesday night in our family room, and I watched as they grew in confidence and assurance, both in themselves and in God.

Giving the gift of time is not easy. It takes sacrifice, but every hour I gave I considered a down payment on their futures. Before long, the youth began to take charge of the study themselves, and I watched as the Holy Spirit developed leadership qualities in them. Another gift that goes along with time is the energy of the Holy Spirit. I discovered early on that if I was going to invest and pour myself into others effectively, it must be done in the power of the Holy Spirit, in total dependence on him.

Because we pastored in that city for over 26 years, I had the privilege of witnessing these young people become adults, choose their vocations and became people of influence in their specific callings.

Sometimes it is financial help that emerging leaders need the most. I have had leaders working with me who needed specific training in a certain area but could not afford the registration cost for a seminar. With the Lord's help, from time to time I have covered the costs, and it proved to be a wonderful investment. The same thing happened to me as a young leader when someone opened doors for me.

Prayer is a powerful way to invest in others. We can pray *for* those we are endeavouring to pour into and we can pray *with* them. An elderly friend of mine, a leader all her life but limited somewhat now by her years, is continually sought out for counsel and prayer in her home. She told me how she was visited by a young couple recently. Before they left, she asked if they would like her to pray for them. When she finished praying, tears were running down their cheeks as they hugged her and thanked her over and over again. In pouring into others, leaders must never underestimate the power of prayer.

As you read these words, are you reminded of people in your life and leadership who poured themselves into you?

Visiting a successful children's pastor recently, I asked, "Who were the people who poured themselves into your life, and what did they actually give you of themselves?" One of the first things she told me was that they were all *real,* people of sincerity and truth; she could trust them. A Sunday school teacher had a strong spiritual impact on her life. She gave her the gift of time in order to encourage her and prayed regularly for her. Her pastor's wife also, although busy with family and church, took time to sit and talk and listen to her. When a great opportunity came her way in high school and she was fearful to take it, her pastor believed in her and her ability and pushed her beyond her comfort zone, helping her to believe in herself.

Asking how she is pouring herself into those she is leading, I was thrilled at how quickly she responded. Working with many volunteers, both youths and adults, she is passing on every type of investment that has been given to her. And the fruit continues to grow.

There is no doubt that it costs to give yourself away, to pour yourself out for others. But that is exactly what Jesus did for the twelve disciples as he trained and taught them. He spent much time with them. He taught them with patience and encouragement. He took risks, sending them out on their own to minister. He passed on what he had been given by the Father, and that is exactly what he desires of us.

REFLECTION

Who poured themselves into you when you were an emerging leader?

Are you looking out for others who may need your investment of prayer and encouragement?

As a leader of a staff, team or organization, how are you giving yourself away? How are you building relationships of trust?

Are you able to be open and vulnerable as you share your story?

Are you leaving a legacy? What will people remember about you?

Part Six
SMART LEADERSHIP

Chapter 15

ORGANIZATIONAL STRATEGIES

Be sure that everything is done properly in a good and orderly
way. (1 Corinthians 14:40, TLB)

Smart leadership is a key to practical wisdom, opening three major
doors: wise organization, wise choice of staff and wise resolution of conflict. A leader with her eyes fixed on the leadership edge cannot afford
to be without this key.

Just a few weeks into a new position, I was overwhelmed. "I will
never make it," I said to myself. "What am I doing in this administrative
role anyway?" A month before, my husband and I had attended a district pastors' conference where, totally unexpectedly, I was nominated
along with a few others for leadership of our district's women's ministry.
I was sure one of the other women would be elected, but to my surprise
my name was the one left on the board after all the votes.

Questions filled my mind. What did the job entail? How many
hours a week? Was it part-time or full-time? I knew the former
director was responsible for sending monthly letters to women's
groups in all the churches. I knew she planned big conventions,
retreats and conferences. She organized all the mission's activities for
the groups and took care of all the financial contributions. The more
I thought about the job, the bigger it seemed. I was dismayed. For
one thing, I could not type, nor had I ever been an event planner, and
I certainly was not an accountant or bookkeeper. Not being one to

give up easily, though, I rolled up my sleeves and decided to make a determined effort.

I signed up for typing lessons with teenagers at a nearby high school and soon began preparing my letters. Before I got the letters out, however, I realized that posters for an upcoming conference needed to be ready and out within the next week. I didn't even have a speaker yet. While trying to get that organized, remittances for missionaries were coming in and needed to be recorded and cheques prepared and mailed out for the monthly support. My head was spinning. How could I keep track of it all? There were too many balls to juggle.

I know my experience was not unique. Most leaders have full plates, brimming inboxes and more emails than they can handle. Scripture says, "Careful planning puts you ahead in the long run; hurry and scurry puts you further behind" (Proverbs 21:5, The Message). Efficient organizing helps leaders bring control over their busy schedules and moves them toward accomplishing their goals with less stress.

ORGANIZE ON A YEARLY BASIS

A wise leader will plan by the year, breaking it down into months and moving her goals along incrementally. She will find a system that works for her so that her annual goals and strategies are moving forward.

Good leaders always have more than they can do. Their schedules are brimful of appointments and commitments. In trying to sort it out, it is easy to put the urgent matters first. They take less time, less energy and less creativity and provide a sense of instant accomplishment. Suddenly, when the most important item rises to the surface, time has run out, and it must be placed on the to-do list for tomorrow.

Organized leaders give their best time to the important matters, regardless of the effort required, placing them ahead of what seems urgent. I must confess that sometimes when I know the important item on my list will require a lot of hard work, I welcome the interruption of the urgent, deliberately procrastinating, stalling for time. But let me stress, regardless of whatever effort is required, high priority goals must come first.

An organized leader is able to work most effectively when her desk is clear of clutter, when her files are organized so she can find things quickly, and when supplies and equipment are conveniently accessible.

One leader shared with me that she stands to take telephone calls. She claims her calls are always shorter. When someone on the other end of the line asks her in the middle of the conversation to "please hold," she tells them she will call back. This takes less time, and time is too valuable to stand and "hold."

A LEADER'S FULL LIFE

> Good leadership is a channel of water controlled by God; he directs it to whatever ends he chooses. (Proverbs 21:1, The Message)

We have looked at organizational strategies for working smart and becoming excellent leaders. In conclusion, I want to discuss the importance of scheduling time and effort in four other categories. First, our time with God—reading his Word, getting to know him, spending time in prayer, talking to him and listening to him. All of our leadership flows out of this close relationship with him. I learned through years of leadership that one of the most difficult things is to make time for consistent, personal devotions in an extremely busy schedule.

Reading Hudson Taylor's biography again (*Hudson Taylor's Spiritual Secret* by Dr. and Mrs. Howard Taylor), I was encouraged by these words: "The hardest part of a missionary career, Mr. Taylor found, is to maintain regular, prayerful Bible study." He followed the exhortation of Andrew Murray in his book *The Secret of Adoration*: "Take time. Give God time to reveal himself to you. Give yourself time to be silent and quiet before him, waiting to receive, through the Spirit, the assurance of his presence with you and his power working in you."

Jesus taught the importance of this discipline. In Mark 6:45, we read that after he had fed the five thousand, he sent the disciples away in a boat to Bethsaida, dismissed the crowd and went away into the hills alone to pray. He needed time to be refreshed in the presence of his Father. And leaders need that too. Because of the demanding responsibilities of leadership and, for some, the responsibility of raising children and caring for household tasks at the same time, women leaders especially find it difficult to be consistent in their devotions. The words in Isaiah 40:29-31 give us great encouragement and hope:

He gives strength to the weary and increases the power of the weak. Even youths grow tired and weary, and young men stumble and fall; but those who hope in [wait upon] the LORD will renew their strength. They will soar on wings like eagles; they will run and not grow weary, they will walk and not be faint.

Leaders must also seek to live healthy lives, getting proper rest, nourishment and exercise. Jesus often spoke to his disciples about rest. "Come with me by yourselves to a quiet place and get some rest" (Mark 6:31). They need to take time off on weekends and holidays to relax, rest and be renewed, physically, mentally and spiritually.

There are times when a leader's family may be neglected. She must set aside times for meaningful interaction with each member of the family. This will take diligence and creativity but will be worth the effort.

A well-balanced life also includes social activities with friends. I have known some leaders who are so engrossed in their ministries or jobs that they have no time for people, no social lives whatsoever. This soon becomes a lonely path. Leaders must go out of their way to make friends and build social relationships. "You use steel to sharpen steel, and one friend sharpens another" (Proverbs 27:17, The Message).

Considering the huge responsibilities of women in leadership, they must learn and employ the strategies of wise organization and careful planning. This is essential if they want to avoid stress and maintain control over their lives. This includes the practical organization of work as well as the wise scheduling of time for personal health and well-being, time for spiritual renewal, family and social life.

SCRIPTURAL GUIDELINES AND CHARACTERISTICS OF A GREAT LEADER

A great leader will exhibit discipline, self control, and faithfulness to God and those they serve.

We find ourselves...able to marshal and direct our energies wisely. (Galatians 5:23, The Message)

I don't know about you, but I'm running hard for the finish line.

I'm giving it everything I've got. No sloppy living for me! I'm staying alert and in top condition. I'm not going to get caught napping, telling everyone else all about it and then missing out myself. (1 Corinthians 9:26,27, The Message)

And this I pray…that you may surely learn to sense what is vital, and approve and prize what is excellent and of real value. (Philippians 1:9,10, AMP)

REFLECTION

What steps will you take to reinforce your organizational skills?

How will you tackle the challenge of the urgent versus the important?

Realizing that excellent leadership flows out of our relationship with God, how will you make time for the important discipline of personal devotions?

What are the other specific areas where you can make beneficial changes, for example, in family, rest, social life?

CHOOSING THE RIGHT TEAM

The best players do not always win the championship,
but the best team does.

I was never an avid hockey fan until I began watching our two sons play Little League hockey. Now, years later, my grandsons head out every Saturday morning for a game. I've learned a lot about hockey. Not long ago, while in Florida, my son took me to a game in Tampa. Excitement—we experienced it. The speed, the strength, the endurance, the teamwork—it was wonderful! It was obvious as the players flew over the ice, with eyes on the puck, that they were also watching each other, ready to assist or respond in a split second. No one was playing the lone ranger, and we watched as the best team won.

When I think of that team and how they worked together, I am reminded of the analogy of the body of Christ that Paul gave in Romans 12:5. "In Christ we who are many form one body, and each member belongs to all the others." "Now you are the body of Christ, and each one of you is a part of it" (1 Corinthians 12:27). Paul explained that each part has a unique role and that the body cannot function properly without each part fulfilling its particular role.

AS A LEADER, HOW DO YOU CHOOSE THE RIGHT TEAM?

LOOK FOR CHARACTER

"Man looks at the outward appearance, but the LORD looks at the heart" (1 Samuel 16:7). God discerns the character of everyone, and character is the most important attribute when choosing members for a team or staff. Character is one's inner force, her moral strength, and includes the qualities that lead to greatness. Leaders should ask the Lord for discernment to see beyond the outward appearance when choosing team members.

Integrity is of utmost importance. It reveals itself in uprightness, wholeness and completeness. A woman of integrity can be believed in, trusted and relied upon. She is true to her word. Honesty and truthfulness flow from her very being. This is a foundational quality to be desired in a team member.

Watch for *faithfulness and dependability*. There are many who possess obvious gifts and talents and appear outwardly to be good prospects, but before long they begin to make excuses for themselves and do not stay with a job until it is finished. Their lack of dependability exposes their unfaithfulness. It is wise to pay attention and to watch for these signs. One who possesses the quality of dependability will follow through faithfully until the job is done.

Be aware of how a potential team member responds to challenging and difficult circumstances. A woman of *steadfast* and unwavering spirit will hold steady and remain true, while one of irresolute character will vacillate, complain and question leadership.

Of highest importance in a team member is a *growing spirituality*. Team members should be women of prayer and the Word. As a team comes together, there will be as many different temperaments and personalities as there are individuals. We cannot assume that unity and harmony will automatically exist in such a diverse group. But that is the goal. I'm encouraged by Paul's example as he wrote to the church at Philippi. Because of their union with Christ, he appealed to them for unity, love, humility and selflessness. He stressed that, because they knew and experienced Christ's love, there should be no complaining or arguing. He encouraged them to put the interests of others ahead of their own (Philippians 2:1-4). This can only happen as believers are growing and becoming more like Christ through prayer and the study of his Word. A team member who is strong in prayer is invaluable to a leader as she seeks to know and follow God's guidance.

CHARACTER TRAITS

In choosing a team, it is important to consider other distinguishing features of character. I call them character traits. *Optimism* is indispensible. Choose women who are optimists. They are positive, cheerful and have a pleasant demeanour. Optimists know how to spread encouragement and create a good climate. They bring out the best in people. Optimism empowers everyone. Optimists possess faith. For example, read about two young men, Joshua and Caleb, in Numbers 13 and 14. They are dynamic examples of optimism. Optimists do not just perceive problems; they find solutions. In a speech at the Lord Mayor's banquet in London on November 9, 1954, Winston Churchill said, "I am an optimist. It does not seem too much use being anything else."

Confidence is another essential trait for a good team member. A confident person exudes faith and trust in God as well as self-assurance. She does not see circumstances as problems but as opportunities to prove God's faithfulness.

Endurance and *perseverance* are two qualities that go hand in hand. Their importance cannot be overemphasized. Certainly in any leadership position there are times when it is necessary to endure hardship and stand up under strain. Scripture speaks of Christ enduring the cross and its shame. He was able to do this because he looked ahead and saw the joy and victory before him. He saw the completion of his work on earth—our salvation—and he saw his return to the right hand of the throne of God in heaven (Hebrews 12:2,3). The hardships of leaders and teams are nothing compared to the pain and suffering of his cross, but he is our supreme example. Leaders must choose team members who possess the strength and fortitude to withstand prolonged stress.

Perseverance was demonstrated clearly to us by the Lord Jesus Christ, throughout his whole life as well as at his death. He came to earth with one purpose, and that was to provide redemption for the human race. There was nothing simple about his birth, his upbringing or his three ministry years. He was despised by his own people. He had no home of his own. His closest friends were simple fishermen, tax collectors and a few humble women. But in Hebrews, we are encouraged to run our race with perseverance, even as he did. Is this too high an attribute to require of a team or staff member? No. Perseverance is the steadfast pursuit of a goal, and leaders should expect, encourage and exemplify such commitment.

The qualities of character and character traits identified here are absolutely essential for an effective and successful team. If a leader is experiencing gaps in her present team, these gaps should be addressed. Personal conversations can be scheduled to discuss the needs. A leader can offer to work with individuals to help them develop strength in their particular areas of weakness. This should be done with much prayer.

COMPETENCY

As a leader begins to put a team together, she will realize that there is a variety of skills and competencies needed. It is wise to make a list of these before she begins to reach out and interview possible candidates. For example, she does not need to have eight women who are excellent event planners but no one who can handle the details and no facilitator who can bring the right people and resources together. She will need a delegator who is able to assign tasks according to skills and experience, and a structure builder, along with a behind-the-scenes person.

Of great benefit will be a spokeswoman who is able to communicate both the vision and practical elements to volunteers, clients, the public and even new team members. A competent administrator is a must. A leader also needs one who shares her passion, understands her heart and can dream with her. There needs to be a servant spirit in each one.

Character, character traits, and competencies—we might call these the "Three Cs" of choosing the right team. If we possess all these and each member is functioning in her unique role, we can expect to have God's blessing and the success he desires to give us.

REFLECTION

Does your present team exemplify the character traits we have discussed in this chapter?

If not, how will you go about changing the situation?

Evaluate the team you are presently working with. Does each one have the qualified skill and experience to function in the position she has been given?

What will be your first step in choosing or changing a team?

RESOLVING CONFLICT

Always put the bridge back in place. They may not walk over it
but you have done what you needed to do. (Unknown)

Conflicts. Crashes. Collisions. As a leader, it is impossible to avoid the combat zone. Resolving conflicts is vital, because if they go on unresolved, they can paralyze a leader. The good news is there are positive, effective methods for bringing about resolution. However, there are also ineffective methods a leader must steer away from.

EFFECTIVE METHODS

Prayer. First and foremost—pray. Ask for God's guidance and wisdom. For Christian leaders, this is absolutely essential as the basis for conflict resolution. "If any of you lacks wisdom, he should ask God, who gives generously to all without finding fault, and it will be given to him" (James 1:5). "I appeal to you…in the name of our Lord Jesus Christ, that all of you agree with one another so that there may be no divisions among you and that you may be perfectly united in mind and thought" (1 Corinthians 1:10).

Slow down. I have discovered that spending hours of time and endless amounts of energy trying to get the other party to see my point of view is futile. My reasoning may be perfectly logical and clear to me, but my friend-in-combat does not understand.

Confidentiality. Make an appointment in a neutral, private setting, perhaps for breakfast or lunch, so you can talk confidentially without being interrupted and without drawing the attention of co-workers. Keep the matter confidential unless you jointly agree to speak to a mutually trusted friend.

Listen with open ears, heart and eyes. This is called active listening. Each person needs to be heard, understood and empathized with. Watch the body language. It often speaks louder than words. Show your understanding of the other person's thoughts and feelings. Give your undivided attention. There is nothing that will end a conversation more quickly than to sense that the person you are talking to is not listening because she is thinking about what she will say next. Your own body language should demonstrate that you are truly interested in what she is saying.

Eye contact is an essential part of active listening also. Everyone has experienced what it is like when someone you are trying to communicate with is looking over your shoulder. You soon get the message "I am not really interested in what you are saying. I have other things and people on my mind." So always give yourself completely to the moment, listening, hearing and being attentive.

Have an open mind. There are times when a conflict arises and you wonder where it has come from. An issue may be brought forward, but you sense there is something deeper, an underlying problem. As a leader, keep an open mind. The overt issue may be camouflage for an unexpressed concern. Ask God for discernment as to the real cause of the conflict. Listen, and show genuine interest in addressing the need.

Bring in a third party. In some situations, it can be advantageous to have a third party listen to both sides of a conflict and then try to help settle it. Success in this case depends on an unbiased third person and the willingness of the two people in conflict to follow the recommendations of the third party.

INEFFECTIVE METHODS

Avoidance. If you are like me, it is sometimes easier to avoid a conflict than to face it head-on, hoping that if you ignore it, it will go away. Sometimes, we may even pretend it does not exist. I have discovered that avoiding and ignoring conflict is not successful and does not produce any resolution. There have been times when encountering conflicts in relationships that I attempted to relieve the tension by showing extra kindness and more friendliness and speaking positive and encouraging words. Once again, I found that trying to smooth things over does not often work.

God's Word speaks specifically to this situation. "If you are offering your gift at the altar [coming to God in prayer] and there remember that your brother has something against you, leave your gift there…First go and be reconciled to your brother; then come and offer your gift" (Matthew 5:23,24). Jesus indicated that we need to *go and be reconciled*, in other words, take the initiative, making every effort to restore a broken relationship and settle a difference.

What about times when our efforts to resolve a conflict are rejected? At these times, we must continue to pray for the other party and keep our own hearts pure.

Withdrawal. Some leaders are tempted to withdraw from a conflict because the timing is not suitable for discussing the disagreement. Others decide that the issue is not important to them and separate themselves from it. Unfortunately, withdrawing often results in breaking the relationship or widening the gap between the two parties. I'm reminded of Jesus' words to "Settle matters quickly with your adversary" (Matthew 5:25).

Aggression. Have you ever had an inner fire boil up within you as you learned of a conflict for the first time? Right away, your reaction is to confront those you feel are responsible and correct the situation, before listening to all sides of the story. As far as you are concerned, the blame is already laid.

An unclear focus. It is wise for leaders in conflict to ask themselves these questions: How am I viewing this situation? Where have I focused the spotlight? Is it on the individual personalities or on the problem itself? Often the personalities become the focal point of a conflict, and leaders find themselves on a detour leading nowhere. A satisfactory solution can only be found as we focus on the problem. If, for any reason, the personalities are the problem, it should be discussed openly, and each party must seek ways to behave differently in order to reduce or resolve the conflict.

HOW CAN CONFLICT BE AVOIDED?

Good communication means less conflict. Good leaders will find that the more and better they communicate with staff or teams, the fewer problems they will have with conflict.

What is good communication? It is more than sending out a typed memo or email. It is more than speaking briefly to a colleague about a matter without allowing time to discern whether or not your intention was actually heard and understood. It is possible for you to mean one thing while the recipient is interpreting your words to mean something altogether different. The best messages you can send will include not only facts but feelings also. Even then, you do not usually get across nearly as much as you are thinking and feeling.

If you are like me, eager, enthusiastic, and anxious to get things done and make things better, you probably speak quickly and try to present all the details in one breath. The listener has no time to consider or digest all the information, and as a result she feels rushed or forced into a decision she is not ready to make. It is important to slow down and present the facts clearly and thoroughly, allowing the listener to digest the information. Actively listen to her questions, and carefully reflect on her thoughts. Then, answer in such a way that she will know she has been heard.

Received communication is what we actually hear and not always what is intended or said. That is why active listening and reflecting are so important. When receiving communication, always use positive body language that lets the speaker know that her thoughts and feelings are being understood. Indicate that you are sincerely reflecting on the issue in the light of her thoughts and feelings.

Real communication happens when the listener is able to respond back to the speaker the message the speaker has intended. You are actually saying, "I got the message; I see your point; I understand your feelings and thoughts." This helps the speaker to know that her feelings of anger, hurt or disappointment have been heard as well as her words. She is then able to move on to resolution.

It is important to use the personal pronoun "I" rather than "you" when explaining yourself. This way it does not seem like you are accusing or fixing blame. Ask open-ended questions to get more information and to clarify the problem, and be willing to change your attitude and to reframe the whole issue if this would lead to resolution.

> There can be no substantial change in a conflict unless both sides move away from a narrow, 'self-interest' point of view. (Dave Toysen, President and CEO of World Vision Canada, *Generosity*)

Resolving conflict is all about communication. Every leader should study and understand the positive and effective methods of resolving conflicts among peers, staff and teams. This will save her from much heartache and grief. She must also be aware of the ineffective methods and the damage they do. But to begin with good communication is even better.

Her communication should include not only facts but also feelings. She should speak slowly and clearly, giving others time to truly hear and consider what she is saying. She will learn to actively listen to what is spoken to her, taking into account body language. When she is able to say "I understand your feelings and thoughts," that is when she acknowledges that she has heard not only the speaker's words but her feelings also. And a resolution is then possible.

REFLECTION

After reading this chapter, how would you describe your method of resolving conflicts?

What steps can you take to work towards resolving a present conflict?

Is there a situation in which changing your attitude would make a difference?

Will you ask God to help you do this?

Part Seven

WHO TAKES CARE OF THE LEADER?

TAKING CARE OF YOURSELF

Be very careful, then, how you live—not as unwise but as wise.
(Ephesians 5:15)

The final key for successful leadership for Christian women focuses on the leader herself. Most leaders are gifted with high energy and drive. They are Type A people who place high demands upon themselves, physically, emotionally and psychologically. Very often they put their ministry or their work ahead of their well-being. So the question is, "Who takes care of the leader?" Who helps her maintain her physical, mental and spiritual health? A leader must not only look after the well-being of her team or staff but also look out for herself. There are five areas to guard if she is to maintain her vitality, vigour and energy and reach her potential.

One cannot have a healthy mind without having a healthy body, because a healthy body provides energy for all areas of life. I recently interviewed several leading women from a variety of professions and callings, including a lead pastor, a children's pastor, an executive manager of an international mission organization, and two professionals—one in education and one in health care. I asked them to describe what they do to sustain the energy they need to carry out their demanding schedules.

At first, some tried to give me the answers they felt I was looking for, but as they opened up and thought about the seven areas that set the course for well-being, they began to realize that there were some areas in their heavily scheduled calendars where they could make even small changes that could have a major impact on bringing balance into their lives. Others were encouraged as they shared their answers, recognizing that they have developed a good balance in all of the important areas.

ELEMENTS THAT BRING BALANCE AND WELL-BEING

In order for leaders to develop balance and maintain energy, I suggest they take inventory of seven critical elements that contribute to well-being.

In your *work*, are you using your unique strengths and abilities? Do you feel you are fulfilling your specific calling? Have you discovered some effective *stress removers*? How about your physical health—*rest, diet, exercise*? Consider your *spiritual development*. Is your spiritual growth keeping pace with your leadership growth? We cannot underestimate the importance of *relationships*. Social connections are essential in the life and development of a leader. These are the seven elements, and it is important to check the balance between them.

A LEADER'S WORK

I was interested to learn that every one of the leaders I interviewed feels her unique gifts and abilities are being used in her work to fulfill her calling, and each one is energized by her work. This is a vital element in the physical well-being of any leader. Several expressed the joy they feel in their work, but one added, "With the greatest joy often comes the greatest stress." Her sense of call keeps her going. As you consider your work, can you say you have a sense of fulfillment? Are your gifts and talents being used and developed? Do you wake up in the morning with anticipation of the day ahead?

Two leaders felt their current opportunities were helping them develop their skills, preparing them for the next steps. One responded enthusiastically, "I'm in the place God wants me at this moment. I'm gaining wonderful experience for whatever he is planning for me next." The young pastor shared how her former ministry role had particularly developed her strong gift of nurturing and helped to guide her into her present pastoring position. Another said that her current ministry is continually growing and expanding, allowing her to develop talents that have been waiting to be cultivated and nurtured.

A leader must be able to look back and review recent years of work, identifying gifts that are maturing and talents that are being developed. It is important also that she is able to look forward and realize that there are opportunities before her for which she is presently being prepared.

PHYSICAL FITNESS: REST

When asking these women about physical fitness, I was occasionally met with a bit of hedging as they discussed such things as rest, exercise and eating habits. One leader reluctantly admitted that she was not good at taking holidays or even taking a day off each week. Deeply committed to her work and having very little administrative assistance, she found herself overworking in order to get everything done to her standard.

Another leader who was energized by her work confessed to working long hours into the night and taking very few weekends off. This kind of schedule provides no stress relief and is threatening to one's health. Energy and vitality may last for a certain length of time, but eventually health is affected, as well as the ability to function effectively as a leader.

Two of the leaders said they had learned to respect the need for rest in order to work efficiently on the job. They have set regular hours for retiring at night and rising in the morning—good advice for every leader. Those who work in offices can recognize the nighthawks (trying to keep awake) by the number of half-empty coffee mugs sitting on the desks.

It is wise for a leader to take time periodically to evaluate and keep a record of her pattern of rest and relaxation. She will soon realize the results and benefits of wise discipline in this regard.

EXERCISE AND STRESS REDUCERS

Exercise is valuable for physical and psychological health. While it builds up the body, it is also great for reducing stress. Most of the women I spoke to are involved in exercise disciplines. Some love to run, outdoors in good weather and on a treadmill in the winter. Others walk regularly. One leader uses an exercise video. Most agree that it is difficult to be absolutely consistent, and they can tell the difference if they neglect a day or two.

Another stress reducer is hospitality and entertaining. It gets one's mind off work and provides opportunities for sharing with friends and building relationships. For several, cooking is a hobby that they thoroughly enjoy. They admit that busy schedules can interfere with their hobby, but they pursue it because of the benefits. Some have other hobbies, such as photography or scrapbooking.

The children's pastor emphasized the importance of guarding her day off. Sometimes she likes to spend it alone, relaxing and being renewed by the quietness, and other times she shares a visit with an intimate friend. A morning at the spa provides stress relief for the healthcare worker, and a spiritual retreat, spent alone, is a regular event for the executive manager. The educator takes Saturday mornings as a time to collect herself after a strenuous week of teaching high-needs students. Staying in her pyjamas for the morning, she takes time to regroup, reassess and relax.

Many leaders acknowledge that they would like to be more involved with a regular routine of exercise and relaxation but argue that they run out of time. They admit to starting exercise programs and soon dropping out because of seemingly urgent interruptions. Time for social activities also falls by the wayside for the same reason. Exercise and stress-reducing activities should be considered as daily or weekly appointments by a leader and scheduled into her calendar.

HEALTHY EATING

We hear a lot of reports today about healthy eating habits. Most of those I interviewed shared their diligence in eating a balanced diet to sustain their energy as well as a sense of well-being. One challenge facing leaders is eating out often in restaurants. A leader should think of this before arriving at the restaurant so healthy choices can be made ahead of time. She should choose veggies and fruit over junk food for snack times.

SPIRITUAL DEVELOPMENT

According to Richard and Henry Blackaby, "More than any other single thing leaders do, it is their prayer life that determines their effectiveness."

How we lead flows out of our relationship with God, out of our personal connection to him. As you read the following stories, do not compare yourself to these women. Be open to how God will encourage you personally and draw you closer to him.

It was thrilling to hear the many methods these leaders use in their spiritual development. The health-care worker volunteers as a teacher in a women's weekly Bible study at her local church and spends three days in study, prayer and preparation for this meeting. Her personal Bible reading often relates to topical studies. She enjoys reading self-help books and authors like John Maxwell and Phillip Yancey.

The educator takes Sunday morning as a time to fast and pray before going to church, in order to gain spiritual grounding for the week to come. In her daily devotional times, she likes to use a devotional book (along with her Bible), for example, Chuck Swindoll's *Great Men of the Bible*.

In answer to my inquiry about her spiritual growth, one woman responded with enthusiasm, "Oh, I love my devotional life." She explained what she calls *Sabbath moments*. If she has read a Scripture in the early morning that has especially blessed her, she will keep her Bible open to that place on her desk, and when she has a free moment she will read it again and meditate on it. Throughout the day it keeps her mind focused on God. She stresses that she could not carry out her spiritual ministry without daily Bible reading and prayer. She enjoys such authors as C.S. Lewis and Dietrich Bonhoeffer. Someone once said, "Leaders should immerse themselves in Scriptures and the writings of great thinkers."

"I am the bread of life. Your ancestors ate the manna in the wilderness, and they died. This is the bread that comes down from heaven, so that one may eat of it and not die" (John 6:48-50, NRSV).

Almost every one of the women keeps a journal. The executive manager explained, "It is like confiding in a friend—who listens." She says it helps her be aware of her heart. Another woman journals her prayers, and another treats her journal more like a diary, reporting after the fact.

RELATIONSHIPS

Why are relationships important? Social relationships help us manage stress. It is comforting to have someone to turn to in difficult circumstances, or even in good times. Relationships with trusted friends help keep us accountable. Some relationships are just plain fun, and we all need that in our lives.

I asked the women to describe the relationships in their lives. A pastor shared that she has a small group of close friends she confides in. She is able to share deeply with them and knows they will pray for her. The educator intentionally connects with staff and colleagues at school. She explained that the classroom is very isolating, and she needs those with whom she can discuss issues, brainstorm and study. Another leader articulated how difficult it is for a single woman in leadership to find opportunities for relationships. In her words, she must actively pursue them. Singles often seem to be neglected or unnoticed.

One of the pastors explained that during a time of transition, after she had moved to a new location, she found it very difficult to establish new relationships. She had left her previous support systems, and in getting settled in the new area, there was little time to spend on making new friendships. It took several months of consistently reaching out to new people, meeting them for lunch or inviting them for a meal, before she felt she had finally built up a small support group. For the healthcare worker, this area poses no problems. Being very outgoing, she builds relationships at her work, in her church and in her community.

A few of the women expressed the importance of their relationships with mentors or friends with whom they can share deeply about their spiritual journeys.

BALANCE

Although each one desires to maintain a healthy balance, the women agreed it takes conscious effort and disciplined action. After our discussions, it was clear that each one knew exactly where she needed to put her efforts.

This has been a look inside the personal lives and habits of several effective leaders. Have you seen a reflection of yourself somewhere? Their stories can be dynamic teachers and encouragers for all who will listen.

REFLECTION

Do you feel that your unique strengths and gifts are being used in your work? Are you energized by what you are doing?

Who are the people in your life who provide care and support? Are you nurturing these important relationships? If not, what steps will you take toward this goal?

How would you describe your rest patterns, your exercise schedule, your eating habits?

Are you strengthened by God's Word and the time you spend in prayer? How can you enhance that part of your life?

Do you have a friend who understands the challenges you face and can walk with you through your processing?

Do you keep a journal where you can express your honest thoughts and prayers?

LEARNING TO SAY NO

Commitments spring up on leaders' calendars like weeds in a garden. (Henry Blackaby)

A leader's daily calendar is already filled with appointments, meetings and deadlines related to her own work, so why does she keep adding new commitments? Many confess that for them saying no is the hardest thing to do, and they end up helping others while their own work gets pushed aside on their priority list. There are several reasons why they might have such a hard time saying no.

For one thing, it is flattering to feel that you are needed in so many different areas and that your expertise is recognized and valued. It makes you feel important and offers prestige. You have an sense that the success of these many extra projects depends on you. Henry Blackaby calls this the "messiah complex." I am sure most of us have experienced this to some degree in our early leadership. As I write, I can remember many times it happened to me before I learned to say the important word—*no.*

I know women who are excellent in their leadership skills yet have fallen into the trap of trying to make themselves indispensible to their organizations. They become key players in every committee and sub-committee, council, board and panel. They rush breathlessly from one meeting to another, feeling very important but complaining at the same time of overwork.

Others find themselves saying yes because they do not want to disappoint people or they feel they may not be asked again. Sometimes people will argue with them if they say no, making them feel guilty, and they do not want to hurt anyone. Some are perfectionists and actually feel they can do everything if they work hard enough.

HOW CAN WE LEARN TO SAY NO?

"And this is my prayer," said Paul, "that your love may abound more and more in knowledge and depth of insight, so that you may be able to discern what is best" (Philippians 1:9,10). He prayed that the Philippians would discern what was best for them. The King James Version reads this way: "That ye may approve things that are excellent." This wisdom Paul teaches indicates that we have choices. We have the ability and the option to choose between the good, the best and the excellent. We decide whether to say "yes" or "no." We must learn to set boundaries.

BOUNDARIES

The most basic boundary-setting word is *no*. There are many who take advantage of a kind and generous spirit. If they are pressed with a need for help, where do they go? They look for the sympathetic friend who is always ready to help. The old saying is certainly true: "If you want something done, ask the busy person."

A young friend of mine recently accepted the position of children's pastor in a large city church. It is her first appointment, and she is full of energy and excitement about her job. Already she is making an impact on the whole church family. Shortly before her arrival on the scene, a youth pastor was hired. Bob is a fine young man but not as organized as Tracy (not their real names).

Shortly after she arrived, Bob began to ask Tracy to help with different aspects of his ministry. She was happy to help at first but soon began to feel that she was being taken advantage of. She noticed that many of the things she was asked to do were because of Bob's lack of organization or his neglect. His work continued to require more and more of her time, and some of her own agenda was being put on hold.

Not knowing what to do, she talked to a mentor, explaining her frustration. She did not want to offend Bob, but she did not know how to say "no." Tracy had to learn that she is responsible for her own work and not that of others and that she must determine her own schedule, with God helping her to set and keep her priorities. She must decide what is important for her and not let anything else crowd it out.

BE PREPARED, PLAN AHEAD

Leaders will always need blocks of uninterrupted time in order to think through and work on significant issues, so it is important that they avoid frequent distractions and interruptions. There are times when phone messages can be left on the answering machine and responded to later. The closed door of a leader's office should be a clear sign that she does not want to be interrupted.

I have found it helpful to mark my calendar ahead, crossing off each day I will need for a project that will require a considerable amount of time. I cross off every day I expect to need during the month, and I am able to say no to anything that would hinder my progress.

I have learned through the years that it is wise when receiving an invitation for ministry or a request for help to not say yes or no immediately. If I reply yes, I am often sorry later. My response now is that I will get back to them in a couple of days (or whatever time I feel I will need to carefully consider). That gives me time to study my calendar and pray about my decision. If the day is free, I make sure that there will be enough time ahead to prepare. Waiting those few days helps me to know in my heart whether to answer yes or no. Some leaders say, "Please let me sleep on it." This is good advice also.

When receiving invitations, a wise leader will be aware of the quantity and the variety and consider what God has called her to be and do. This will dictate her primary response. She will have self-awareness and know if the invitation matches her call. This self-knowledge and awareness comes with maturity and directs her response.

A leader's calendar is a good indication of her wisdom and dependence on God's guidance. It reveals her ability to choose what is good and excellent and whether she is able to set wise and clear boundaries. It will be evidence of her ability to plan her time in advance, taking into account her own priorities and God's guidance.

REFLECTION

In reviewing your calendar, are there some unnecessary commitments stealing valuable time for more important things?

What steps will you take to change this?

Have you set boundaries for your time? How did you do it?

How will you begin to plan ahead so that you have more control over your schedule?

SAFEGUARDS FOR WOMEN IN LEADERSHIP

Be careful what you think; your life is shaped by your thoughts.
(Unknown)

Maintaining safeguards is a vital key in the hands of Christian women in leadership. These safeguards are based on biblical principles and practical wisdom. We read in Scripture that God's divine power has given us everything we need for life and godliness as we get to know Christ personally and intimately. He has promised us faith, good character, spiritual understanding, self-control, perseverance, godliness, warm friendships and generous love. As we possess these qualities in increasing number, Peter tells us, we will be effective and productive as we grow in him. He adds that if we do these things we will never fall (2 Peter 1:3-11).

SUPPORT AND GUIDANCE OF FRIENDS

Practical wisdom tells us it is important that a woman in leadership does not try to lead as a *loner*. She needs a group of at least two or more trusted supporters who can help her maintain perspective and offer guidance when she is under pressure. This group will be there when she needs someone to talk to and to provide an outlet for anxieties. They can also function as an accountability group for her, which is absolutely vital.

JOURNAL KEEPING

Many leaders do not recognize the benefits of journal keeping. A journal is like a true friend. Journaling is like writing a prayer. One can pour out fears and frustrations, uncertainties and doubts, or can confide about failures and consider how to address them. Amazingly, the writing will often stimulate new insights and understanding. It may be based on a Scripture passage she has read or the words of a friend. Clarity and wisdom will illuminate her mind.

This happened hundreds of times in the life of King David. Just read his songs. Most of them begin with David crying out because of difficult and hopeless situations, but before his lament is finished, he is suddenly singing, rejoicing because God has reminded him of his great faithfulness in the past and revealed how he will help him in the future.

POSITIVE ATTITUDE TOWARD FAILURE

All humans make mistakes, and God uses people who fail. Mistakes can be stepping stones leading to success if they are used as learning opportunities. Wise leaders learn from mistakes but do not dwell on them. They make decisions, make mistakes, and then move forward.

GUARD YOUR TIME

Time is valuable and can easily be squandered by uninvited interruptions, too many breaks and lengthy phone calls. It slips away quietly, moment by moment, without even being noticed. Disorganization can contribute to an irretrievable loss of time, resulting in lack of balance between work and home life. Many leaders find themselves with little time for family and friends, exercise or social life. The results of this imbalance can be disastrous. Moses prayed, "Teach us to number our days aright, that we may gain a heart of wisdom" (Psalm 90:12). It is paraphrased in *The Message* as "Oh! Teach us to live well! Teach us to live wisely and well!"

RESIST PRIDE

"Pride goes before destruction, a haughty spirit before a fall" (Proverbs 16:18). There is a temptation for leaders to take credit for the successes and achievements that really belong to an entire team or staff. Pride drives them to seek the spotlight when the accomplishments are the result of teamwork and the blessing of the Lord. Jesus spoke plainly to his followers when he said, "Apart from me you can do nothing" (John 15:5). The credit does not belong to one person alone. The attitude of pride in a leader is demoralizing to those who have spent time and energy on a major project. When a leader takes all the glory, it suggests she has no appreciation or esteem for her team, and their respect for her soon diminishes. Scripture is clear on God's attitude toward pride. "God opposes the proud but gives grace to the humble" (James 4:6). "Do not be wise in your own eyes; fear the LORD and shun evil" (Proverbs 3:7).

AVOID SEXUAL TEMPTATION

Every woman in leadership needs a group of at least two or more personal accountability partners who will share openly and honestly and be unafraid to address issues in the leader's life that concern them.

Women in leadership must set an example of integrity. They must remember that the men they work with are not their personal friends or their confidantes. They are colleagues. They must remain professional, not confiding or discussing personal matters with them or listening to their personal stories. Unprofessional communication may appear very innocent in the beginning but quickly opens the door for temptation. Many leaders, both women and men, have had their ministries, careers, families and reputations destroyed by succumbing to sexual temptation. Remaining professional in all communication helps a leader to avoid this tragic pitfall.

Another important safeguard for a married woman in leadership is to cultivate and maintain a strong, healthy marriage. It is wise for her to listen if her husband expresses legitimate concerns about her relationships in the workplace. There may be situations where no matter how hard a wife tries to strengthen a marriage, her husband does not respond. In cases like this it is even more important for the woman to have a good accountability group. One woman in this kind of situation explained to me that when she was promoted to a new position where all of her colleagues were male executives, she made a commitment that she would be true to God and to her husband, in spite of the lack of support she received from him.

I have interviewed many women in leadership who said that because of awkward circumstances they have been placed in on occasion, they have made a conscious decision to protect themselves from these compromising situations. If possible, they ensure that there is a window in their office. They avoid travelling alone in a car or plane with a man. They prefer to drive themselves to meetings and make their own flight arrangements. When being met at airports, they request to be picked by at least two people. This habit of avoiding compromising situations and protecting oneself from temptation was followed resolutely by Billy Graham, carrying him safely through half a century of a high-profile ministry.

AVOID OVER-FAMILIARITY

Over-familiarity with staff can create difficulty for a woman in leadership. She must remember that because of her position of leadership, she is wise to keep her professional life separate from her private life. Because women are sensitive and nurturing, this is sometimes difficult. However, over-familiarity can sabotage her authority and effectiveness as a leader. It is better to choose friends and build relationships outside of work so her personal life is kept for that audience.

MAINTAIN A STRONG SPIRITUAL LIFE

Therefore I urge you…in view of God's mercy, to offer your bodies as living sacrifices, holy and pleasing to God—this is your spiritual act of worship. Do not conform any longer to the pattern of this world, but be transformed by the renewing of your mind. (Romans 12:1,2)

Paul urged the Christians in Rome to dedicate themselves wholly to the Lord—their eyes to see as he sees, their ears to hear his voice, their voices to speak for him, their hands to serve as Christ served and their feet to follow in his steps, their hearts to be tender as his is tender and their minds to be transformed into his likeness.

Practical safeguards that are so important for a woman in leadership come in many forms. It may be through trusted friends and supporters, mentors or an accountability group. It may be inspired as we put our thoughts on paper in a journal. God's wisdom comes as we turn our failures into learning opportunities, enabling us to move forward into success.

The spiritual life of a leader is foundational to every area of her ministry or work. A woman's daily devotional life of Bible reading and prayer is the most essential and strongest safeguard possible for her entire scope of ministry. God's Word speaks forcefully about the sin of pride and its consequences. It is equally strong in its counsel regarding avoiding sexual temptation. "Submit yourselves, then, to God. Resist the devil, and he will flee from you" (James 4:7).

REFLECTION

Who are the trusted supporters you can go to when you need someone to listen and offer counsel?

Do you have a group that will hold you accountable in your walk with God?

Does your journal keeping affect your spiritual life? Describe what you have learned.

What methods do you find most successful in guarding your time?

How do you keep pride in check?

What safeguards have you established to help you resist sexual temptation?

Conclusion

JOURNEY TO THE LEADERSHIP EDGE

You have just explored the pathway to the leadership edge. In the pages of this book, the stories and examples of women in leadership, women just like you, have inspired and challenged you to be the leader God calls you to be. Biblical characters, historic figures and present-day leaders have joined the procession, passing through obstacles and trials, celebrating joys and victories, always pressing forward. You have received seven keys—keys to guide you on this exciting journey to the leadership edge.

Passion is the first key to successful leadership. Do you remember the moment God called you? Can you recall his quiet voice speaking to you through circumstances or his gentle touch on your shoulder, pointing the way to go? Does the wonder of his call still thrill you? Does it bring tears to your eyes? Does your heart burn with the vision he gave you— with the glimpse of *the big picture?* With the key of passion, you will impart this vision to those who are looking to you for leadership. Your commitment, steadfast perseverance and tenacity of purpose, along with well-defined goals for your strong staff, will equip you to lead at the edge.

Credibility, both spiritual and personal, is the second leadership key. Your personal credibility is the absolute and essential foundation for your leadership. Integrity in words and actions determine credibility and define character. Honesty above all ensures that other qualities will thrive, qualities like truthfulness, self-discipline, dependability, loyalty and perseverance. Effective spiritual leadership flows out of your relationship with God. The most important element in building spiritual credibility is prayer. As you spend time with God in prayer and in his Word, you will lead with influence and power, through God's presence in your life.

Inspiration is the key to motivation, that ability to pass your vision on to others with persuasive enthusiasm. Inspiration contains the energizing quality of optimism and the igniting influence of personal "presence."

There is no key more vital than *courage* for moving leadership to the edge. Courageous leaders never give up. They know what it is to persevere, to keep pressing on, even in the midst of difficulty and prolonged stress. *Endurance* is a word they live by. Christ set the example, and leaders who are determined to go to the edge follow his lead. Like him, they keep focused on the goal.

I especially love the fifth key—*nurturing*. As you mentor and pour yourself into others, you can open doors for them to reach their highest potential. As a nurturing leader, you have the privilege to influence and provide opportunities for others to move into leadership themselves.

The sixth key opens up the important and practical skills of wise organization, resolving conflict and choosing the right team. Each of these skills, if handled wisely, will increase your effectiveness as a leader and pave the way toward the leadership edge.

The final key focuses on the leader herself. While it is the last, it is not the least in importance. It is vital that we ask the question, "While the leader is serving and ministering to others, who cares for the leader?" Pay attention to the guidelines, because they are signposts on the path to *the leadership edge*.

Seven keys to successful Christian leadership for women—I encourage you to study and apply them to your life and leadership. Over several decades I have discovered their power in my travels throughout Canada and around the globe, teaching and encouraging women to become influencers and shapers of the world. Take hold of the keys. Strive for excellence. Follow your heart, and God will use you in ways beyond what you can even "ask or imagine" (Ephesians 3:20).

CASTLE QUAY BOOKS

OTHER CASTLE QUAY TITLES INCLUDE:

Walking Towards Hope
The Chicago Healer
Seven Angels for Seven Days
Making Your Dreams Your Destiny
The Way They Should Go
The Defilers
Jesus and Caesar
Jason Has Been Shot!
The Cardboard Shack Beneath the Bridge
Keep On Standing
To My Family
Through Fire & Sea
One Smooth Stone
Vision that Works - **NEW!**
The Beautiful Disappointment - **NEW!**
Bent Hope - **NEW!**
Red Letter Christian - **NEW!**

BAYRIDGE BOOKS TITLES:

Counterfeit Code: Answering The Da Vinci Code Heresies
Wars Are Never Enough: The Joao Matwawana Story
More Faithful Than We Think
Save My Children - **NEW!**
What the Preacher Forgot to Tell Me - **NEW!**
To Be Continued: The Story of the Salvation Army in Woodstock - **NEW!**

For more information and to explore the rest of our titles visit
www.castlequaybooks.com